Higher Education in the 21st Century:
GLOBAL CHALLENGE AND NATIONAL RESPONSE

IIE Research Report Number Twenty-nine

Higher Education in the 21st Century:

GLOBAL CHALLENGE AND NATIONAL RESPONSE

Edited by

PHILIP G. ALTBACH
Boston College

and

PATTI McGILL PETERSON
Institute of International Education and
Council on International Exchange of Scholars

April 1999

Institute of International Education
and
**Boston College Center for International
Higher Education**

ISBN 087206-252-X

This book is available from
IIE Books
Institute of International Education
POB 371
Annapolis Junction, MD 20701-0371
www.iiebooks.com
800.445.0443 tollfree
301.617.7804 phone
301.206.9789 fax

Contents

Preface

ALLAN GOODMAN

More persons will attend colleges and universities in the next century than in all of human history. Most of the capacity to accommodate this demand is yet to be built, and most of it will be built outside the United States. This book presents the thinking of leading higher education researchers and policymakers around the world about what kinds of blueprints are needed and who will be the architects for those future higher education systems and structures. The essays grew out of papers presented at a December 1998 symposium, "Global Challenge and National Response," sponsored by the Rockefeller Foundation and convened by Dr. Patti McGill Peterson, executive director of the Council on International Exchange of Scholars (CIES), which in affiliation with the Institute of International Education (IIE) administers for the U.S. Information Agency the Fulbright Fellowship Program. The conference benefited greatly from the advice and participation of Philip G. Altbach, J. Donald Monan, S.J. Professor of higher education at Boston College and director of its Center for International Higher Education, who served as editor and copublisher with IIE of this publication, which is the 29th in a series of IIE Policy Research Reports on current issues in international education exchange.

The IIE plays many roles in the development of human capital around the world, through administration of federally funded graduate programs like the Fulbright and Humphrey fellowships, delivery of more targeted professional training through USAID's Global Training for Development, and promotion of university linkages through Information Exchanges focused on key world regions (Southern Africa, East Central Europe, North America). Most of these activities mobilize and share the expertise of U.S. higher education institutions, extending these resources to academics and policymakers abroad.

Over 600 higher education institutions around the globe are members of IIE, sharing information on developments in their institutions and world regions through IIE's on-line and printed newsletters and website. Through IIE's Professional Exchanges Program, hundreds of International Visitors each year participate in study tours (with support from USIA), learning how U.S. higher education institutions grapple with issues ranging from financing, to the changing profile of the undergraduate, to the impact of new technologies, to the aging of the professoriate.

But even as we share with others the well-developed U.S. higher education model, that model is under serious review at home and is in a period of dramatic transition. Other countries are facing similar transitions, and under even greater pressures to respond to changing national needs, with shrinking national resources. With Rockefeller Foundation support, this symposium and resulting publication are the beginning of what we hope to be a sustained dialogue among key actors involved in "global capacity building" and the development of higher education systems, including those who design and fund activities, those who shape and staff these institutions, the students and employers served by the institutions, and those who conduct research on their effectiveness. The purpose will be to assess the relevance of current models to 21st century needs at different stages of development around the world, and to consider how these models might better incorporate and reflect changing assumptions about and vehicles for human capacity development.

As Vaclav Havel so aptly observed, we live in an era in which everything is possible and nothing is certain. The future is also happening faster than any of us can imagine. These conditions predominate in world politics largely because power is being dispersed not only across nations but across cultures. Education is the medium of that exchange. The participants in the symposium and subsequent publication share a common vision that, in the words of the late Sen. J. William Fulbright, "We must try, through education, to realize something new in the world— by persuasion rather than by force, cooperatively rather than competitively, not for the purpose of gaining dominance for a nation or an ideology but for the purpose of helping every society develop its own concept of public decency and individual fulfillment." They have formed an informal network that will continue to share information and provide support as their higher education systems grapple with common problems and undergo their individual transformations.

These transformations are as needed today as when the Senator wrote about them in 1977. The universality of the dollar, the English language, and the Internet makes us all think we are closer than, in fact, we are. And, it turns out, virtual exchange is no substitute for what we are all working to achieve: the broadening of a young person's cultural horizons, the increasing of their capacity to think and work globally, and the creation of opportunities for them to participate in making the world a less dangerous place. This publication, we hope, will extend the dialogue and exchange of views to a broader audience and engage new voices in this vital shared enterprise.

Introduction

PHILIP G. ALTBACH and PATTI McGILL PETERSON

Higher education worldwide and its future direction are neither simple nor straightforward topics, yet they are the focus of this volume. To address such complex topics, we have assembled a distinguished group of commentators from five continents to reflect on the current state of higher education and the prospect of its future evolution. These thoughtful analysts have taken as their starting point the theme chapter in this volume. The themes presented in this chapter were chosen for their growing significance in many countries and regions of the world. They constitute the starting point for our respondents' reflections and are meant to elicit their experience in different parts of the world as well as their own points of view. The result is a thoughtful mix of context and perspective that will, we think, advance our understanding of likely future scenarios for higher education. We have no crystal ball that will provide an accurate portrayal of future global developments in higher education. We are convinced, however, that this set of comparative views will help us understand the basis for future trends principally because our analysts bring such a well-informed spectrum of analysis to the topic.

A comparative perspective can seldom provide us with detailed prescriptions for action, but it permits us to expand our horizons. In higher education, where we are so often bound by the constraints of national thinking, a comparative perspective is especially valuable because academic institutions worldwide stem from common traditions, and the issues facing higher education around the world have many common characteristics. The purpose of this volume is to provide such a comparative perspective.

This book stems from a symposium sponsored by the Institute of International Education in Washington D.C. on December 3, 1998. The chapters here were prepared for this symposium, and revised extensively as a result of the discussions and further comments. We are especially indebted to our respondents, who prepared insightful analyses and worked with us on revising them for publication. The Center for International Higher Education at Boston College assisted in the organization of the symposium, and is responsible for providing editorial and publication support for this book. Financial support from the Rockefeller Foundation, with additional support from the Institute of International Education, made the symposium and this volume possible.

1.
Global Challenge and National Response:
NOTES FOR AN INTERNATIONAL DIALOGUE ON HIGHER EDUCATION

PHILIP G. ALTBACH and TODD M. DAVIS

Higher education has profoundly changed in the past two decades, and those involved in the academic enterprise have yet to grapple with the implications of these changes. Academic institutions and systems have faced pressures of increasing numbers of students and demographic changes, demands for accountability, reconsideration of the social and economic role of higher education, implications of the end of the Cold War, and the impact of new technologies, among others. While academic systems function in a national environment, the challenges play themselves out on a global scale. We can learn much from both national experiences and international trends. Ideas and solutions from one country or region may be relevant in another.

Since academic institutions worldwide stem from common historical roots and face common contemporary challenges, it is especially appropriate that international dialogue take place. A comparative and global approach to thinking about higher education benefits everyone—the experience of one country may not be directly relevant to another, but

issues and solutions touch many nations. This essay has several key aims:
•   to highlight issues in higher education that face many countries and about which an international discussion can contribute insights;
•   to contribute to the internationalization of higher education through discussion of international initiatives and linking of people and institutions committed to a global perspective and expanded international programs;
•   to create a network of colleagues and centers working in the field of higher education worldwide in order to foster ongoing dialogue, communication, and possible collaborative research; and
•   to link policymakers, key administrators, and the higher education research community in a creative dialogue on the central issues facing contemporary higher education.

We see this essay, and the discussions that we hope it will stimulate, as a first step in an ongoing discussion. We are especially concerned to link North and South in a discussion that has for so long been dominated by the industrialized countries. We are convinced that there is much that can be learned by considering the experiences of countries and systems worldwide.

Background and Global Perspective
While it may not yet be possible to think of higher education as a global system, there is considerable convergence among the world's universities and higher education systems. The medieval European historical origin of most of the world's universities provides a common antecedent. The basic institutional model and structure of studies are similar worldwide. Academic institutions have frequently been international in orientation—with common curricular elements and, in the medieval period, a common language of instruction—Latin. At the end of the 20th century, English has assumed a role as the primary international language of science and scholarship, including the Internet. Now, with more than one million students studying outside their borders, with countless scholars working internationally, and with new technologies such as the Internet fostering instantaneous communications, the international roots and the contemporary realities of the university are central.

Higher education systems have also been moving from elite to mass to universal access, as Martin Trow pointed out in the 1960s. In North

4

America, much of Europe, and a number of East Asian countries, academic systems approach universal access, with close to half the relevant age group attending some kind of postsecondary institution and with access increasingly available for nontraditional (mainly older) students. In some countries, however, access remains limited. In China and India, for example, despite dramatic expansion, under 5 percent of the age group attends postsecondary institutions. In some countries with relatively low per capita income, such as the Philippines, access is high, while in some wealthier nations, it remains a key point of challenge. Throughout Africa, access is limited to a tiny sector of the population. Access is an increasingly important issue everywhere, as populations demand it and as developing economies require skilled personnel.

Demands for access come into conflict with another of the flashpoints of controversy of the present era—funding. Higher education is an expensive undertaking, and there is much debate concerning how to fund expanding academic systems. Current approaches to higher education funding emphasize the need for "users" to pay for the cost of instruction, as policymakers increasingly view higher education as something that benefits the individual, rather than as a "public good" where the benefits accrue to society. This new thinking, combined with constrictions on public expenditures in many countries, have meant severe financial problems for academe. These difficulties come at a time when higher education systems are trying to provide expanded access. Higher education's problems have been exacerbated in many of the poorer parts of the world by the idea, popular in the past several decades and stressed by the World Bank and other agencies, that basic education was most cost-effective—as a result, higher education was ignored by major lending and donor agencies. Now, higher education is back on the agenda of governments and multilateral agencies just as academe faces some of its most serious challenges.

Academic systems and institutions have tried to deal with these financial constraints in several ways. Loan programs, the privatization of some public institutions, and higher tuition are among the alternatives to direct government expenditure. In many parts of the world, including most of the major industrialized nations, conditions of study have deteriorated in response to financial constraints. Enrollments have risen, but resources, including faculty, have not kept up with needs. Academic infrastructures, including libraries and laboratories, have been starved of funds. Less is spent on basic research. Conditions of study have deteriorated in many of the world's best-developed academic systems, including Germany and France. Students have taken to the streets in large numbers to protest declining budgets and poor conditions for the first time since the 1960s. There has also been a dramatic decline in academic conditions in sub-Saharan Africa and in some other developing areas.

While these trends, and the circumstances discussed below, vary to some extent from country to country, there is considerable convergence. Academic leaders worldwide worry about the same set of topics. Specific conditions vary from one country to another, and there are certainly major differences between the Netherlands and Mali. Yet, solutions from one country may be relevant, at least in terms of suggesting alternatives, elsewhere. For example, there is much interest in Australian ideas concerning a "graduate tax"—a repayment scheme based on postgraduate income. The United States, as the world's largest and in many respects leading academic system, experienced the challenges of universal access first, and American patterns of academic organization are of considerable interest elsewhere.

We live in a period of rapid change in higher education, a period when we can learn much from the experience of others. In short, higher education has gone global but with a variety of accents. These global concerns or issues are actually not discrete topic areas. They are better understood as issue clusters. Each of the following are actually related concerns that are increasingly difficult to isolate and manage in a reductionist manner. A discussion of the short list of issue clusters follows.

The Issue Clusters
We identify several themes that seem to us to be central to current developments in higher education worldwide. These themes deserve elaboration and analysis. They affect countries and regions differently, although we believe that all are relevant internationally, and that a discussion of implications can lead to understanding that will be useful for both comparative and national analysis.

• Education and work are activities that should feed one another. The links and transition points from initial education to the work force are weakly articulated. This is true in the developed world as well as in the developing world. Educators and business leaders rarely discuss, let alone agree upon, a set of skills and orientations that are prerequisites for successful employment. The formal structures by which education systems prepare students for tomorrow are similarly weakly developed. Models developed in Germany, through the linking of postsecondary education and apprenticeship arrangements, or the U.S. community college system are currently being explored in several areas. Professional education often links well to employment in many countries, but education in the arts and sciences is less well articulated. It is not clear how close an articulation is possible, but the issues are worthy of further consideration.

• While the initial transition from school to work may be poorly articulated, the demand for education throughout the life cycle is becoming apparent. Fed by rapid changes in technology and the creation of employment categories that did not exist 10 years ago, workers and employers must continually attend to the educational dimension. As the nature of work has evolved, so have the needs of those in the workforce to continually upgrade their capacities. This has led to the development of a variety of educational forms beyond the bachelor's degree. In Germany, recent changes in the degree structure have led to the modularization of graduate degrees. In the United States, certificate programs and short-term courses of study are being rapidly developed. By one recent estimate corporations in the United States alone will spend $15 billion over current expenditures by 2005 just to maintain current employee training levels. Others estimate that worldwide expenditures on training amount to many billions of dollars annually to ensure that their workforce has the skills necessary to compete in an ever-competitive and high-velocity business environment. In many countries, especially in the developing world, graduate education is coming into its own as the need for advanced skills and for continuing education becomes increasingly clear.

• It has become a point of banality to remark on the changes that technological developments have wrought. Indeed, many of the dislocations in school-to-work transition and the press for lifelong education are partially the result of these developments. More directly, however, technology has made possible a revolution in distance education that has important implications for the accreditation of educational institutions and assurance of quality in such circumstances. Technology is also beginning to have an impact on teaching and learning in traditional universities. It is also a truism that this technology is expensive, subject to rapid obsolescence, and requires high initial investment simply to get into the game. For many developing countries, cost is at present prohibitive, and it is precisely these areas where technology can provide the greatest short-term improvement. Technology is also central to the communication, storage, and retrieval of knowledge. The traditional library is being revolutionized by web-based information systems, as are the management systems of many universities. Technology is the least understood of the issue clusters discussed here, and perhaps the one with the greatest potential for transforming higher education.

• We have noted in passing the increase in the number of internationally mobile students. While this is an exciting and important trend, it is not without some serious consequences. As the market for individuals with transnational competencies has grown, so have opportunities for individuals with marketable skills in other countries. Currently, the transfer of talent has been from developing countries such as India and China to the developed world. In the United States, the stay rates for advanced students in the engineering disciplines and the sciences can be higher than 75 percent for students from particular countries. From the perspective of national education authorities, these students may represent a considerable hemorrhaging of talent that has been developed by the students' countries of origin. If nations are to develop, a means must be found by which talent can flourish in the soils that originally nurtured it. Related issues of internationalizing the curriculum and providing a global consciousness to students, including instruction in foreign language, and ensuring that the academic profession is linked internationally are central to any discussion of the internationalization of higher education.

• Although seldom discussed, one of the areas of greatest expansion worldwide has been graduate education—the postbaccalaureate training for the professions as well as for science, technology, and teaching. Graduate education offers great opportunities for international links and cooperation. Countries can take advantage of graduate training capacities elsewhere, and the new technologies can provide key links. Highly specialized and advanced-level teaching and research deserve careful analysis.

• The privatization of higher education is a worldwide phenomenon of considerable importance. In Latin America and some parts of Asia, the fastest-growing parts of the academic system are private institutions. In Central and Eastern Europe, private initiative is also of considerable importance. Public universities are in some places being "privatized" in the sense that they are increasingly responsible for raising their own funds. They are asked to relate more directly to society. Students are increasingly seen as "customers." The expansion of the private sector brings up issues of quality control and accreditation since in many parts of the world there are few controls as yet on private-sector expansion. Access is also a central issue. As some developing areas, such as sub-Saharan Africa, will soon be experiencing the growth of private institutions, understanding in a comparative context the problems and possibilities of private higher education is an urgent need.

• The academic profession is in crisis almost everywhere. There is a rapid growth of part-time faculty members in many countries, and traditional tenure systems are under attack. The professoriate is being asked to do more with less, and student-teacher ratios, academic salaries, and morale have all deteriorated. The professoriate is being asked to adjust to new circumstances but is given few resources to assist in the transition. Without a committed academic profession, the university cannot be an effective institution.

• Access and equity remain central factors, but in the current policy context are sometimes ignored. While academic systems worldwide have expanded dramatically, there are problems of access and equity in many parts of the world. Gender, ethnicity, and social class remain serious issues. In many developing countries, higher education remains mainly an urban phenomenon, and one that is reserved largely for wealthier segments of society. Although women have made significant advances, access for women remains a serious problem in many parts of the world.

• Accountability is a contemporary watchword in higher education. Demands by funding sources, mainly government, to measure academic productivity, control funding allocations, etc. is increasingly a central part of the debate on higher education. Governance systems are being strained, sometimes to the breaking point. To meet the demands for accountability, universities are becoming "managerialized," with professional administrators gaining increasing control. The traditional power of the professoriate is being weakened.

•   Expansion brings with it increased differentiation and the emergence of academic systems. New kinds of academic institutions emerge, and existing universities serve larger and more diverse groups. In order to make sense of this differentiation, academic systems are organized to provide coordination and the appropriate management of resources.

These are some of the key topics that affect contemporary postsecondary education worldwide. While this is by no means a complete list, it provides the basis for discussion and cooperation. International and comparative analysis can help to yield insights on how to deal with these topics in individual countries.

2.
Global Challenges and Chinese Responses

MIN WEIFANG

Chinese higher education has a long tradition. Ancient Chinese higher education dates back three thousand years, to the Zhou Dynasty, and flourished in the Han Dynasty, two thousand years ago. It was then called *taixue*, which meant highest institution of learning. However, the modern Chinese higher education system is the result of learning from and in interaction with the West, sharing common historical roots with higher education in other countries, as stated in the theme chapter. Thus, to a certain extent, Chinese higher education institutions, as do universities in other countries, face similar contemporary challenges, resulting from the advancement of science and technology, economic growth, social changes, and the internationalization and globalization of the world economy, as well as of higher education.

However, one has to be aware that Chinese higher education institutions respond to common challenges in a specific institutional context, characterized by the transition of the Chinese economy from an ossified, centrally planned system to a dynamic, socialist market economy. This transition has led to a series of profound socioeconomic changes and has had a strong impact on almost every aspect of Chinese higher education. Currently, Chinese higher education enrolls about 6 million students, in some 2,217 institutions (1,107 of these are adult higher education institutions), under dozens of different central ministries and provinces that segment the higher education system. While the economic sector took the lead in the reforms, dramatic changes have taken place in the human resources sector. It is the labor market, and no longer central planning, that plays the fundamental role in shaping human resources development and allocation. The overspecialized and departmentalized higher education system based on the rationale of a planned economy no longer works well in the new market context. Thus, it was imperative to change the rigid central planning system of governance and administration and to establish a new institutional framework and operating mechanism for the Chinese higher education system, according to the logic of the newly developed market economy. This is a tremendous task, encompassing a series of reforms, which includes breaking the departmental boundaries between different government agencies that segmented the higher education system; reorientation of the government/university relationship; and revision of the legal status of higher education institutions to grant universities more autonomy and enable them to respond to the needs of socioeconomic development as signaled by the labor market, rather than as dictated by government planning. The role of the state will be changed from one of direct control and management to one of regulating universities within a solid legal infrastructure and financing higher education with priorities, providing policy guidance and coordination, and monitoring and evaluating higher education institutions. In recent years, dramatic changes have been taking place in this direction. The new system has just started to take shape, but is far from being institutionalized. One has to understand the dynamic nature of current higher education development in China and view the key issues discussed in the following sections within this changing institutional context.

Articulation of Education and Work
As in other parts of the world, how to improve the link between education and the workforce represents a serious challenge for Chinese universities. School and work in China used to be articulated by a central planning mechanism, through government job assignment—a system that is changing, although it is still functioning to some extent. Designed to serve a planned economy, the centralized job-assignment system created serious problems for both graduates and employers. It was impossible for governmental planning agencies to obtain accurate information about what the millions of students are studying in the many different colleges and universities, nor could they know in detail the actual manpower needs of thousands of employing units. The situation

was worsened by the many overly complicated bureaucratic procedures and rigid formalities between graduates and employers, who usually did not meet one another before the employment decisions were made. The graduates had little say in what they would do but had to accept the job-assignment decisions of the government, and employing units had little freedom to select graduates but had to accept those assigned to them. Both were dominated by the government plan. It very often occurred that vacancies could not be filled by persons with the proper expertise and that graduates trained in particular skills had to be transferred to jobs requiring different qualifications. According to a survey of 100,000 college graduates a few years ago in China, more than 40 percent had a job unrelated to their training.

Along with the deepening reforms since the 1980s, the economy has become more and more dynamic and market oriented; the employing units gained more and more autonomy in their operations and became more conscious of cost-benefit and cost-effectiveness analyses in human resources utilization; the open door policy and technology transfers have led to a rapid renewal of technology in industry. More importantly, the nonstate sector, including private enterprises and joint-venture companies, has emerged and quickly expanded, hiring and firing according to production needs and without any consideration to the government job-assignment plan. These new developments have resulted in a rapidly changing pattern of manpower needs and human resources allocation and utilization. More and more graduates enter the labor market to find jobs on their own. The articulation of school and work has gradually shifted from a central planning mechanism to one based on the labor market. However, this is only a partial solution to the problems. The labor market mechanism is not a panacea for the articulation of school and work. Because of the imperfections of the market and the lag in market effect, market failures do occur from time to time, even in those countries with a long tradition of a market economy—as well as in China, whose market economy is still very immature. Recently, there have been more reported mismatches of supply and demand in the labor market, and some graduates have been unable to find jobs closely related to their training. In addition to providing better career and employment counseling, Chinese universities need to coordinate their programs more effectively with the actual manpower needs of the country by establishing close links with employers. The job-placement ratio of graduates is one of the important indicators of institutional effectiveness in the market context. The state should still have a role to play in improving the articulation of school and work—for example, by providing policy guidance and information services. It seems that to tackle the challenge, universities, business, and government will have to work together more closely.

Access and Equity

The fast-growing market economy, the rapid development of science and technology, and rising individual income levels and living standards have stimulated the ever-increasing demand for higher education opportunities. The Chinese higher education system has expanded very quickly over the past 18 years. Enrollments in higher education institutions rose from about 1 million in the early 1980s to 6 million in 1998 (including 2.8 million enrolled in adult higher education institutions). However, the expansion of higher education has not kept up with the demands. Currently, higher education enrollments account for only 7 percent of the college-age population in China, which is very low by international standards. The world average now is about 13 percent, while the industrialized countries enroll more than 30 percent of their college-age cohort. Access to higher education is one of the most challenging issues facing the Chinese government.

The distribution patterns of the limited higher education opportunities can result in social equity problems. Ethnic minority students have been given favorable terms for admission to universities. They accounted for 6.83 percent of the total enrollment in 1997. Given the fact that minority groups account for a similar proportion of the total population, they are reasonably well represented in Chinese higher education. Female students accounted for only 37.3 percent of enrollments; thus they are underrepresented. College admissions decisions rely mainly on performance on the national competitive examinations. Thus, students from families of higher socioeconomic status, who have the advantage of better learning conditions, are usually overrepresented in the student population, although measures have been taken to support students from low-income families. No statistics are available on this subject. Probably the most serious equity issue concerns the regional disparities. To deal with the huge unmet demand for higher education, local governments have been mobilized for higher education development. However, since China is a geographically large country, characterized by very uneven development among the different areas, regional disparities are obvious. For example, the number of college students per 10,000 population in 1997 was 323 for Beijing, 165 for

Shanghai, and 146 for Tianjin, while it was only 29 per 1,000 for Guangxi, 26 for Qinghai, and 20 for Guizhou. The expenditure per student also varied widely from region to region: 12,127 yuan in Beijing; 12,687 yuan in Shanghai, 7,919 yuan in Guangdong, but only 4,869 yuan in Anhui, 3,678 yuan in Sichuan, and 3,861 yuan in Guizhou. The increasing regional disparities in higher education development have drawn the attention of the state. Central interventions have been made, such as intergovernmental grants allocated to underdeveloped regions. However, since these disparities are rooted in the uneven socioeconomic development among regions, including differing financial capacity and labor market needs, the disparities still prevail. How to tackle the problems represents a major challenge in China.

Financial Constraints
As in most of the countries in the world, if one surveyed the university presidents in China, they would point to shortages of funding as their greatest headache. While higher education expanded very quickly, the increase in state appropriations for higher education could not keep up with the growing costs. The unit allocation per student in constant terms has actually declined since the mid-1980s. Thus Chinese universities have been faced with increasing financial constraints since the mid-1980s. Although the costs for salaries and fringe benefits have accounted for an increasing share of the total budget, faculty salaries are still relatively low. The government has responded to faculty complaints about low income levels with some pay increases, but the increases were quickly offset by inflation. This situation has resulted in an unstable teaching force. Many faculty members have left the teaching profession. Since a growing proportion of funding goes to salaries, there is a serious shortage of both nonsalary instructional funds and the necessary facilities and equipment for higher education institutions. This has resulted in understocked laboratories and libraries. Many higher education institutions have had to cut their subscriptions to periodicals that they had had for many years. Obviously, without successfully tackling the financial constraints, the Chinese higher education system will be unable to sustain a healthy development in the coming century. Proposed strategies include enhancing management to improve institutional efficiency and effectiveness in resource utilization, making greater efforts to increase state allocations, granting universities more autonomy for revenue generation, and adopting cost-sharing and cost-recovery policies—such as raising tuition fees, coupled with student loans and scholarship programs. The implementation of these changes

involves many policy changes and has significant social consequences. Thus, as in many other countries, the task is a very challenging one.

Changing Patterns in the Provision of Higher Education
The tremendous demand for higher education opportunities and the constraints of limited public resources for the expansion of public higher education have led to a flourishing of alternative institutions—called *min-ban* higher education institutions, which means "non-state-run" or "run by the local people." According to international standards, these Chinese *min-ban* institutions are private in nature, but people in China prefer the term *min-ban*. The development of these *min-ban* institutions is driven by labor market demand. When employers needed certain types of skills from college graduates and the public institutions could not meet these needs, some individuals came up with programs to fill these manpower gaps. While public universities charge only about 20 percent of the unit cost per student in tuition, *min-ban* institutions charge 100 percent of the cost. In 1994, the Chinese government formulated and promulgated the "Regulations on the Establishment of *Min-Ban* Higher Education Institutions." In the past few years, about 1,300 *min-ban* higher education institutions have been established, among which only about 20 were officially accredited and recognized by the national authorities. Even these 20 institutions are usually allowed only to issue certificates or diplomas for two- or three-year programs. None are allowed to grant academic degrees—such as bachelor's, master's or doctor's degrees. Currently, these institutions primarily offer low-cost programs in the humanities, the social sciences, management, accounting, and law. They are able to be very flexible and adaptive in their programs. If managers for hotels, restaurants, and the tourist industry are in short supply, these institutions quickly set up relevant programs. When there is an oversupply of accountants in the labor market, they cut back on their accounting programs. They hire a large number of part-time teachers and retirees from public universities. Thus these new institutions are also very unstable, and far from being well established. There is still no systematic policy framework or solid legal infrastructure for private higher education, nor are any official statistics available about these *min-ban* colleges. The statistics bureaus simply ignore their existence. Given the huge unmet demand for higher education and the limits on the expansion of public higher education, the private provision of higher education will definitely be one of the most important policy issues that China will face in the coming century.

The Impact of Technological Development

The advancement of science and technology, especially the revolution in information technology—which has significantly reduced the costs of processing and disseminating knowledge—has dramatically changed the world economy and higher education. Indeed, as argued in the theme chapter, in China people have already felt the strong impact of advances in information technology on the school-to-work transition, lifelong education, distance education, etc. Even Chinese thinking on the role of universities is changing: in today's world, no one can deny the fact that a country's capacity to generate, accumulate, deploy, and utilize knowledge and information is critical for development. Along with the evolution of the world economy toward a knowledge-based system, higher productivity and economic growth rely increasingly on the successful integration of innovation, processing, dissemination, and application of knowledge. As knowledge-based institutions, universities, through their teaching, research, and various services to industries and societies, can play this integrating role. As argued by Manuel Castells, if knowledge and information are the electricity of the new world economy, universities are one of the power sources on which the development process of the 21st century has to rely. This proposition is borne out by some cases of successful development—such as the Stanford-Silicon Valley model in the United States. Chinese universities are moving in this direction. One example is Peking University's Founder System, which seeks to integrate teaching, research, and industrial development. The issue is how to formulate systematic policies and strategies to assist universities in playing a more significant role in the development process of the new world economy of the 21st century. It is a real challenge for China, as well as for other countries.

3.

The Transformation of an Imperial Colony into an Advanced Nation:

INDIA IN COMPARATIVE PERSPECTIVE

SUMA CHITNIS

The theme chapter in this book argues for an international dialogue on the challenges and problems that confront higher education worldwide because, although they are presently dealt with as purely national issues, both the problems and their solutions have serious global implications. It further asserts that an intercountry sharing of experience is vital even to country-level deliberations, because the challenges faced by different countries are basically the same, and practically all countries are served by systems of higher education with common roots. The similarities are clear, and are articulated in the theme chapter. It is also the case, however, that important national differences render easy comparisons impossible. Nonetheless, the distinctiveness of the experience of different countries should, in fact, be used to understand the challenges and the problems in depth and to deliberate together on solutions.

The distinctiveness of the Indian experience, as presented in this chapter, lies in its history as a developing country. It also lies in the paradox that the university system, on which the country now depends for its advance as an independent nation, was initially designed to function as an instrument of colonial rule. This chapter briefly describes colonial higher education, specifies how the objectives of higher education in independent India are the opposite of the objectives of colonial higher education, offers a brief a glimpse of the balancing act involved in achieving the new objectives, and tries to present some globally relevant lessons from the Indian experience.

Higher Education as an Instrument of Colonial Rule
The European system of higher education was introduced into India by the British, in 1857, with the establishment of universities for European education in Bombay, Calcutta, and Madras. Although modeled after the University of London, these universities were not meant to be institutions for the advancement of knowledge, or full-fledged centers of higher learning. The British government had established them with two limited objectives: first, to introduce the Indian elite to European culture, and thus, to colonize the country culturally; second, to produce a cadre of Indians equipped to serve the British administration in India and to practice the professions of law, medicine, and teaching, as required by the British.

All the three universities, as well as 18 others that had been established by the time India acquired independence from British colonial rule in 1947, were designed to serve these limited objectives alone. They were, therefore, different from their European counterparts. For instance, only disciplines such as history, philosophy, literature, the languages, law, medicine, and education, considered relevant to the two objectives, were taught. The social sciences, as well as technical and technological subjects, were neglected. Facilities for studying science were restricted to the level required to produce school teachers and undergraduate-level college teachers. Facilities for graduate education and research—even in fields such as medicine and law—although considered essential, were practically unavailable. Those who aspired to graduate qualifications or specialization were expected to go to Britain for further education.

The emphasis on imbibing European culture and knowledge was so pronounced that universities never really encouraged a spirit of critical inquiry or independent thinking so vital to the advancement of knowledge. India has an old tradition of knowledge and learning; in fact, a well-established system of higher education functioned as early as 1000 B.C. In this system, the construction of knowledge, the beliefs on which knowledge is based, basic concepts, and the organization of learning are very different from the European tradition. But the system is validated by the fact that it sustained Indian civilization for centuries. Initially, the British had accepted the indigenous system of knowledge, and allowed institutions for indigenous education to exist. But with the establishment of the first three universities, the British declared their preference for European knowledge, instituted policies that favored European education, and withdrew their support for indigenous institutions. English was established as the only medium of instruction permitted for university education. British economic policy, similarly, withdrew support for indigenous crafts, skills, and professional practice, although India was highly advanced in fields such as textiles, architecture, waterworks, and medicine. Together, these two policies steadily created a climate in which indigenous knowledge was rejected and links with traditional learning were broken.

Access to higher education was restricted because facilities were meager. In addition, British policies were self-consciously elitist. Whenever it was asked to expand facilities, the British government would argue that the benefits of privileges provided to the elite would eventually trickle down to the masses. Elitism was also encouraged by the fact that instruction was only available in the language of the rulers.

Universities were statutory bodies closely controlled by the government. Their structure and functioning were governed by a university act passed by the government. The governor of a province was the chancellor of all universities within the province under his jurisdiction. He appointed the vice chancellors, who were second in command and directly in charge of individual universities. Government nominees sat on the all-important bodies—such as the Senate, the Executive Council, the Academic Council, and committees for the selection of faculty and administrative staff.

The Indian Response
Indians valued European higher education as the means to acquire employment in the British establishment; to enter the professions of law, medicine, and teaching as practiced under British rule; and to gain access to European social circles. They valued the English language

as a window on the Western world. And they acknowledged the fact that European education had inspired the nationalist movement for freedom. But they felt that policies pertaining to university education in India denied Indians the opportunity to advance, distanced them from their own culture, restricted economic growth, and bred continued dependency on Britain for knowledge. The determination to free university education in the country from all these handicaps shaped nationalist dreams and aspirations for higher education in independent India.

When India acquired independence, education was chosen to be the principal instrument for the country's transformation from a poor, dependent, economically and technologically backward imperial colony into an advanced nation. In the larger design for this transformation, which calls for economic development as well as extensive social and political change, higher education was charged with two major responsibilities. First, higher education was to provide the manpower required for economic growth and for an efficient delivery of services such as healthcare, transport, communication, and community welfare—considered basic to a developed society—and to contribute to the advancement of knowledge in the manner required to place India on par with the developed world. Second, higher education was to function as an instrument of equality. It was recognized that these objectives were the very opposite of those that universities in British India had served. Nevertheless, it was believed by instituting appropriate policies and facilities it would not be difficult to gear universities to the new objectives.

The Production of Manpower and the Advancement of Knowledge
In order to enable them to advance knowledge and to produce the manpower required, universities in independent India have been equipped with facilities for undergraduate as well as graduate education, in the full range of disciplines available at universities in developed countries. At least one agricultural university has been established in each state. In addition, a new category of national-level apex institutions—such as the Indian Institutes of Technology (IITs) and the Indian Institutes of Management (IIMs)—have been established to provide world-class education in fields such as engineering, technology, management, and medicine, which are considered critical to development. Several national-level institutions have also been established for research in different fields. All these new institutions have been established in consultation and with assistance from some of the best-

known experts and institutions of higher learning in Europe and North America. The government has, thus, invested heavily in revamping higher education.

India no longer depends on developed countries for higher education or for qualified manpower. It has the world's third-largest pool of scientifically and technically trained personnel. The products of Indian higher education are accepted for employment worldwide. Students from other countries, particularly the African countries, come to India for higher studies. Research, which was altogether absent in British India, is now well established.

Until about two decades ago there was euphoria over all this. However, since then, serious problems have surfaced. For instance, highly qualified Indians, particularly the products of prestigious institutions such as the IITs, have been migrating to Europe, North America, and recently to Australia. Although referred to as the "brain drain," this phenomenon was initially celebrated as India's successful entry into the international market for employment. But it is now resented that, while the migrants prosper, the country is deprived of returns from its massive investment in technical, technological, and professional education. Institutions of higher education, particularly the apex institutions, are blamed for their failure to cultivate, among their students, a commitment to serve the country.

Even more serious is the problem of the underemployment and unemployment of graduates. This phenomenon is generally explained away with the statement that the economy has not grown at the pace, and on the scale, required to absorb all the manpower that the institutions of higher education produce. Yet, many positions in industry, in government administration, and surprisingly even in educational institutions, lie vacant for want of suitably trained persons. This is in part because qualifications for employment are narrowly and rigidly defined. But it is also due to a measure of mismatch between what higher education produces and what the country needs.

The Needs of the Traditional Sector
The most disturbing aspect of this mismatch is that the products of the country's system of higher education are not adequately equipped to serve the traditional sector. This sector consists of occupations such as agriculture, farming, fishing, forestry, indigenous crafts, services,

and trades, and accounts for 70 percent of the economy. Fifty years ago, when India chose massive industrialization as the strategy for economic advance, it was believed that this sector would simultaneously modernize. But this has not happened. Occupations in this sector depend almost entirely on indigenous knowledge, skills, and technologies and traditional modes of marketing and management. It is now pointed out that the economic advance of the country hinges precariously on the development of this sector and that its knowledge, technology, skill, and manpower needs, hitherto neglected, must be urgently addressed.

The experience of some nongovernmental organizations (NGOs), that have made considerable headway in this direction indicates that addressing these problems is not easy. It shows that technologies transferred from developed countries need considerable adaptation before they work satisfactorily in this sector. Moreover, the people in this sector are unwilling to give up traditional methods and practices, particularly because many of these are deeply entrenched in sacred beliefs and customs. By interacting patiently and establishing rapport with the people, these NGOs have been able to enrich traditional skills with modern technologies and bring about substantial change. It is significant that they in turn have come to understand and appreciate the wealth of wisdom, experience, and knowledge underlying traditional practices and ways. But firmly anchored in Western technology and thought, unused to interactive learning and teaching, and bound by structural requirements that are highly inflexible, university teachers and researchers in India have been finding it difficult to relate to this sector.

Much the same happens with respect to the task of advancing knowledge in music, dance, philosophy, psychology, yoga, Ayurvedic and Unani medicine, architecture, astronomy, and a number of other fields where rich stores of knowledge and traditions of learning, banished by the British, now lie waiting to be revived and developed. Distanced from indigenous knowledge for more than a century, universities have been finding it difficult to relate to it.

Keeping Pace with Global Advances and Market Forces
While higher education is thus challenged from the grassroots and by the indigenous culture, it is also relentlessly pressed to keep pace with global advances, in the development of both manpower and research.

Faced with the competing demands on its resources, the government is unable to provide adequate funds to maintain facilities at the level required—even at institutions such as the IITs and IIMs, internationally recognized for the quality of education.

There are other problems. For instance, in order to make their mark in their disciplines, Indian academics prefer to do research and to publish on issues that are of international import. These issues are not always relevant to the country's needs. In the international network, they are often exploited by being invited only to provide data from the Indian subcontinent. Meanwhile market-driven demands force institutions of higher education to concentrate on the short-term objective of providing employment-oriented courses, at the cost of their mission to advance knowledge. Because there are few careers in research, very few good students opt for courses that lead to the advancement of knowledge. While the academic purpose is thus relegated to the background, there is no room for a good all-round liberal education either.

More recently, with the liberalization of the country's economy, global market forces have generated new fears and dilemmas for higher education in India. In order to take advantage of the low cost of educated labor, multinationals have been locating many of their labor-intensive operations here. While institutions of higher education are pushed to produce appropriate manpower, observers are unsure about whether this will contribute to the country's economic progress or toward its colonization by the economies of the developed world.

Higher Education as an Instrument of Equality
To equalize access, the bottom line of the government's policy is to provide opportunities for higher education to all those who aspire to it. To serve this commitment, facilities have been massively expanded. Fees have been kept low. The vernacular languages have been introduced as the media of instruction. Several universities offer fee waivers to women students. Further, in a bold move to extend access to sectors of the population known to have poor access to university education, the government has instituted a policy of "reservations." According to this policy, it is mandatory for all institutions of higher education that receive government funding (and almost all do) to reserve a quota of admissions as well as faculty and administrative positions (a) for the castes that are considered to be low in the caste hierarchy and that were therefore traditionally denied the right to education, and (b)

for the aborigines or tribes who were traditionally excluded from education because they functioned outside the mainstream of urban and rural life. Scholarships and other facilities have also been liberally provided for these two categories.

Together, all these provisions have yielded spectacular growth. In 1950–51 when the country's First Five Year Plan was launched, there were 27 universities serving 174,000 students. By 1997 there were 229 universities, more than 8,000 colleges, 6.4 million students, making India's system of higher education the second-largest in the world. To finance this expansion, the Government of India has consistently increased its share in the total expenditure on higher education—from 49.1 percent in 1950–51 to more than 90 percent today, although government allocations to education have declined to 3.8 percent of GDP, the lowest in South Asia.

It is significant that despite these impressive statistics the enrollment in higher education in India today accounts for barely 6 percent of the relevant age group, as compared to 30 percent in Europe and 50 percent in North America. This is partly because the expansion has been offset by the growth of the population in the relevant age group. Nevertheless, the fact illustrates how difficult it is for developing countries to bridge gaps and to keep pace with the developed world.

The Pressure of Numbers and the Decline in Quality
Although they have been increased phenomenally, facilities fall short of demand. For some professional programs, there are more than 500 applicants per seat. The unrest this generates is so intense that in some states the government has had to administer admissions. To meet the demand, facilities are constantly stretched beyond capacity. As a result, quality suffers. For instance, when classes were small, teachers were able to encourage questions and stimulate interaction, in spite of teaching by the lecture method, extensively used in the country. But now, as they lecture to large numbers, this is no longer possible.

Quality is also affected by the fact that few students are academically motivated. Most pursue a degree for the status it carries and because it is a required qualification for employment. Students in the professional stream take courses that are relevant to their future work, and regardless of their initial attitude, many grow to be interested as they move on. But more than 70 percent of the students are enrolled in the traditional faculties of arts, science, and commerce, in courses that have little relevance to the occupations they will eventually take up. They are aware of this and therefore indifferent, certificate oriented, and examination driven, as are their teachers. Meanwhile, institutions are weighed down by the bureaucratic requirements of the government and their own rules and regulations, designed to cope with large numbers. As the academic purpose has thus receded in importance, malpractice and corruption have grown. Professional education, hitherto relatively safe from these forces is being slowly sucked in.

New Inequalities and the Transformation of the Structure of Opportunities

While quality and relevance thus suffers, equality does not fare any better. In fact, new inequalities have emerged. Professional education has steadily grown in prestige. Among professional institutions, the new apex institutions such as the IITs and IIMs are considered to be in a class apart. It is significant that the students who succeed in the competition for admission to professional courses in general, and to these institutions in particular, largely come from more well-to-do, educated homes and superior schools.

The privileges of wealth are visible in the fact that both private colleges that charge hefty fees and European, North American, and Australian universities that peddle expensive courses have no dearth of students. Another sign is the fact that parents who can afford to do so send their children abroad for further education. Until recently, this happened after completion of the first degree. Now, as quality declines and admission to better institutions has become highly competitive, many students are sent abroad for the first degree.

The effort to provide equal opportunities for higher education is also defeated by the fact that facilities for schooling are highly uneven and unequal. Most significant is the fact that barely 65 percent of children in the relevant age group complete primary school and that less than 30 percent complete high school.

Reservations have enabled the disadvantaged castes and tribes to advance significantly, in education as well as in employment, but they have become highly politicized. For instance, the performance level of candidates admitted to reserved seats at institutions such as the IITs is significantly lower than the cutoff point for open admissions, but attempts to bridge this gap with remedial courses are rejected as discriminatory. In Parliament these institutions have been accused of trying to maintain international standards at the cost of addressing national realities. And most institutions of higher education are neck deep in litigation over reserved admissions, as well as reservation of faculty and administrative positions.

In the face of this scenario, higher education in India can hardly claim to have functioned successfully as an instrument of equality. Yet there is visible, as well as statistical, evidence of a complete transformation of the structure of opportunities in the country—for the traditionally disadvantaged castes and tribes, for women, and for the classes that not very long ago had little or no access to higher education, and to the futures that education opens up.

Government Policy on Privatization
The expansion of higher education has been criticized and questioned, given the associated academic and social costs. But the government is unwilling to retreat from its initial promise, regarded by it as the realization of the nationalist dream and as part of its basic obligation as the instrument of a welfare state. In a more pragmatic vein, the government recognizes that people's aspirations for higher education are so intense that it would be suicidal to curb access. It is also driven by the ambition to achieve enrollments comparable to those in Europe and North America. This ambition is legitimized by the fact that bodies such as the World Bank consistently emphasize the high rates of return from higher education. Finally, there is also the consideration that by expanding opportunities to improve qualifications it is able to contain the frustrations in society because of underemployment and unemployment.

However, faced with public demand and political pressures to accomplish universalization of primary school education (which was to have been achieved by the end of the Second Five Year Plan, in 1961) at least by the end of the century, the government has finally realized that it cannot afford to subsidize higher education as it has for the last 50 years. At the same time, a section of the population clearly has the capacity to pay for the expensive higher education facilities provided by some private institutions and by foreign universities. The government is, therefore, considering privatization. However, it has two apprehensions. First, equality might be placed in jeopardy if the facilities available to those who are able to pay are superior to the facilities available to those who cannot pay. Second, higher education could be commercialized to the point that it is almost entirely market driven. The government is, therefore, thinking of extending a system already in operation in some states during the last decade.

A large number of institutions of higher education in the country are owned and managed by private bodies. Most are "aided" with government funds that fully cover the costs of their maintenance and operation. Regardless of whether they are aided or unaided, all private institutions charge the same fees. Moreover, in academic as well as administrative matters, all of them are very closely controlled by government and university rules and regulations.

According to the system in place in some states, referred to earlier, selected and preferably new private unaided institutions are allowed to charge substantially higher fees. However, the amount has to be approved by the government. The selected institutions are given a few concessions in administrative matters. But, by and large, they are closely governed in the same manner as are other institutions. It is unfortunate that India is considering this brand of privatization—one that does not allow for the space, flexibility, and freedom required for the advancement of knowledge, quality, and relevance.

Conclusion
There is much to learn from the Indian experience, particularly for developing countries, for countries served by European education but rooted in non-European cultures, and for countries making the transition from a fully state-supported education system to one being serviced by the market. A number of lessons can be drawn from the experiences presented in this chapter.

European higher education implanted in non-European societies has often smothered or displaced indigenous knowledge, technologies, skills, values, and other elements of the indigenous culture. Developing societies with non-European cultures are now beginning to discover that it is not wise to anchor plans for development in European knowledge and technology alone. It is now recognized that indigenous knowledge, once dismissed as primitive, has much that is of global value, and deserves to be retrieved.

The market is a powerful force in making higher education relevant to employment. But like a cancerous growth, it can destroy love for learning, crowd out philosophical and literary pursuits, stifle the advancement of knowledge, and render both theoretical and liberal education irrelevant. With the globalization of the economy, the developed societies tend to impose their manpower needs on the higher education systems of less-developed societies and to push the latter into the background. These problems have to be consciously addressed.

The internationalization of higher education, generally understood as the intercountry exchange of students and faculty, has many other facets: the growth of an international market for educated manpower and the challenge to equip students with transnational competencies so that they can compete in this market; international partnerships and networking for the advancement of knowledge; the phenomenon of individual scholars as well as individual countries promoting their vested interests to the disadvantage of the larger endeavor; and the marketing of courses by universities in countries other than their own and consequent issues of ownership, partnership, accreditation, acceptability, and accountability.

The Indian experience clearly indicates that the traditional organization of higher education into disciplines—particularly in the faculties of the arts, commerce, and science—has become largely irrelevant to the knowledge and skills needs of society. It reveals that higher education needs to be in close touch with the world of work and to interact with it meaningfully. It also illustrates that much that is vital to the advancement of knowledge and technology is happening outside the system of higher education. Higher education systems must find a way of linking to these developments. In several other ways, the Indian experience underlines the need to restructure higher education and to do this as part of restructuring the larger framework of secondary education, and with full awareness of societal realities and needs.

The Indian hesitation in the matter of the privatization of higher education indicates that the challenge for the country is to function as a civil society and to substitute civil control for regulation by the state. The current situation with respect to the privatization of higher education in India illustrates the anxieties of the transition. These are a few of the lessons from the Indian experience that are pertinent to an international dialogue.

30

4.
Higher Education in Africa:
CHALLENGES AND STRATEGIES
FOR THE 21ST CENTURY

GEORGE S. ESHIWANI

At a recent Association of Commonwealth Universities (ACU) conference in Ottawa, Canada, Mwalimu Julius Nyerere, the doyen of African
politics, stated that it is not possible to clone Western democracy and
capitalism like Dolly the sheep. At the same conference the secretary
general of ACU, Michael Gibbons, said that emerging universities within
the Commonwealth should avoid the pitfall of wanting to become another Cambridge or University of California. While the university will
certainly seek to establish its own identity in the 21st century, it should
not be forgotten that nearly all the modern universities in sub-Saharan
Africa have been 20th century extensions of metropolitan university
models in the various colonial countries of Europe.

Partly because these models are no longer valid in a rapidly changing
continent and are outmoded in their countries of origin, the university
in Africa must strive to create new paradigms in order to respond to the
numerous socioeconomic challenges of the 21st century.

Some of the main issues that are likely to dominate the discussion of
higher education in Africa in the next millennium are: the effects of
demographic changes on the provision of higher education; the adverse effects of a deteriorating economy on quality education; the par-

ticipation of institutions of higher learning in the production and ownership of knowledge—especially in the area of information technology;
and the role of universities in the political and cultural changes that are
likely to occur in the 21st century.

This chapter offers a brief historical note regarding the development of
higher education in sub-Saharan Africa in the last 40 years or so, and
then discusses the challenges and strategies facing the region.

Historical Background
The history of modern universities in Africa is a short one, dating back
about 40 years after most African countries attained independence in
the 1960s. There were, however, a few colleges in sub-Saharan Africa
that provided postsecondary education earlier than that. For example,
Makerere in Uganda and Yaba in Nigeria offered postsecondary education in the 1930s. The pattern of development was such that most of
the emerging African universities were modeled after established British or French universities. In the 1960s and 1970s, the focus of most
African universities was on institution building, concentrating mainly
on development of manpower for leadership positions, creation of new
relevant degree programs, development of local textbooks, and staff
development.

The challenges facing most African countries at independence with
respect to university education were threefold: first, the university was
viewed as a vehicle for training high-level manpower for the new nations. In this regard there was a need to expand the system, both in
numbers and in the degree offerings. For example, in Kenya, within a
period of 30 years (1964–1994), the country established five public
universities and several private universities. Second, the "new" African
university, was expected to adopt the best of the past tradition of
academia and search for universal knowledge and truth, while responding to the real problems, needs, and aspirations of the new nations
(Ishumi 1994). Third, the university in Africa was seen as the driving
force for economic development. However, apart from providing high-
level manpower for both the public and private sector, it is hard to find
concrete examples of universities in Africa playing a leading role in the
development of the economies of their countries.

The turmoil that gripped the continent a decade into the independence
period—displacement of persons due to wars, famine, devastating

weather conditions, sociopolitical instability, and student unrest—decelerated the motion of many universities toward the achievement of their stated missions. Most of these problems have persisted into the 1990s with adverse effects on institutions of higher learning.

Challenges and Strategies

As the present century draws to a close, social pressures and the specific requirements of the labor market have resulted in an extraordinary diversification in universities and in programs of study. University education has not been exempt from the force and urgency with which educational reform is politically advocated as a response to the economic imperatives. Universities no longer have a monopoly on higher learning. In this regard, it is imperative that the university in Africa continues to demonstrate its relevance to local problems. In doing this it must be both the repository and creator of knowledge; and it must become the principal instrument for passing on accumulated experience, cultural and scientific, for socioeconomic development.

Expansion

The main pressure being put on universities in Africa today include rapid expansion in student enrollments despite dwindling financial provision. The pace of expansion over the past 20 years has been enormous, as evidenced by the number of institutions of higher learning—especially in Nigeria, Kenya, Uganda, and Tanzania. The number of professional faculties and departments in all universities also showed a corresponding increase in sub-Saharan Africa. The demand for higher education is also illustrated by the number of African students seeking to attend universities in the United Kingdom, the United States, and India. While the expansion enabled training of much-needed manpower in the earlier days, the current growth exceeds the capacity of African economies to meet the high demand for university education. Strategies to cope with the expansion problem must therefore be sought.

Expansion in enrollments has enabled university education to move from elite to mass access; as a result, universities in Africa have become more and more open. The elitism observed among the preindependence graduates—"School Certificates talking only to graduates and graduates only to God" (Ishumi 1994, 63)—is no longer present. The geometric rise in the number of students enrolled in universities in Africa is best illustrated by the situation in Kenya. There, enrollments in public universities rose from a mere 400 students in

1964, at the time of independence, to slightly over 41,000 students in 1997. Due to the population explosion, the demand for university education far exceeds the capacity of the public universities. Nearly 150,000 students take the national examinations at the end of secondary school. Of this number, about 80,000 apply for university admission. Nearly 30,000 candidates meet the minimum university entry requirement. The maximum capacity in the public universities is 10,000. This works out to be about 7 percent of those who complete secondary school education. Private universities established mainly by religious groups fill the gap left by the public universities and in part meet the demand for tertiary education. Two problems that the private institutions seem to be precipitating are encouraging moonlighting by professors and lecturers from the public universities and contributing to the imbalance between science- and arts-based programs. Whereas public universities have reduced this imbalance to a ratio of 45:55, private universities are reversing this trend by concentrating their course offerings on arts-based courses.

Equity and Access

Regrettably, women have not benefited proportionately from the dramatic expansion of higher education. The proportion of women in African universities is as low as 20 percent in several countries. The low percentage of women's participation shows that the continent is underutilizing more than 50 percent of its available human talent. In Kenya, despite the enormous expansion explained above, inequalities persist in access for female students from the arid and semiarid parts of Kenya. The Joint Admissions Board—the board that deals with university admissions in Kenya—has created special criteria to address this problem. African universities must understand that the empowerment of women through education would contribute to all areas of development and determine to a large extent the pace of development on the continent. Universities face the challenge of ensuring the participation of women in higher education both as students and professionals. Universities in Africa must offer an environment in which women can function effectively.

Higher Education Finance

Expansion of student numbers in African universities has been achieved without a proportionate rise in the resources available to higher education. Universities face the task of raising the funds that will enable the institutions to meet the demand for the expansion and improvement of educational opportunities. As a result, most universities have experienced funding crises over the last decade. In Africa, this is partly due to structural adjustment programs, partly due to policies that encouraged free tertiary education, and partly due to poor financial management practices. To meet this challenge, Kenya, for example, has established the Commission of Higher Education, which coordinates policies on university education; introduced payment of tuition and accommodation fees by students; and established the Students Loans Board to assist students from poor social backgrounds. Financial constraints have led the universities to introduce school-based programs for teachers (at Kenyatta University) and parallel degree programs (private) at the University of Nairobi and Makerere University in Uganda. These programs enable universities to raise extra funds. Universities must also learn to use existing resources more efficiently and find cheaper ways of operating. Involvement of the private sector in financing higher education could also be intensified.

The nonperforming economies of African countries have not only affected the operation of local universities but have also greatly reduced the migration of students from Africa to universities in Europe and America. In a world that is fast moving toward globalization, this could be a dangerous trend for Africa.

The Issue of Brain Drain
The loss of talented staff—brain drain—has become one of the critical issues facing African universities. In the past, qualified staff would not return to their home institutions after obtaining higher degrees from universities abroad. In recent years, African universities have watched qualified staff move to other African universities, especially in the south. Studies have shown that it is the highly trained and experienced staff who leave in search of greener pastures. African universities face the serious problem of retaining their trained staff through intellectual and monetary incentives. In the 21st century, the issue of brain drain must be addressed because it creates a continuing need for staff development and has negative effects on training and research.

Information and Communication Technology
Information technology is the science of collecting, storing, processing, and transmitting information. The above tasks are accomplished through computer networking, which has spread rapidly in sub-Saharan Africa during the last decade. As a result, most African nations have

established connectivity through computer networks. However, universities in Africa face serious constraints related to the cost of using computers as a means for information exchange. In 1996, the World Bank came up with the concept of the African virtual university (AVU). AVU is a concept of distance education, which uses a technological mode of instructional delivery. The main objectives of AVU are to improve the quality and relevance of science, engineering, and business instruction in sub-Saharan Africa; raise the enrollment levels in these areas; and support and encourage African universities to develop, on a competitive basis, a curriculum that could be broadcast to other African countries. AVU is currently implemented in six African countries: Kenya, Zimbabwe, Uganda, Zanzibar, Ethiopia, and Ghana. Several other countries will soon join the project. The AVU project is perhaps the only project in Africa that enhances international cooperation in higher education at the regional level (Africa) and a global level, by collaborating with institutions—mainly in the United States and Canada. For the participating universities, the AVU project has helped to solve one of the major problems facing researchers and scholars in African universities: namely, lack of up-to-date journals and accessibility to information from other libraries. The digital library is a giant step forward for these universities. For example, Kenyatta University, in Kenya, where the AVU project first started, is currently able to access more than 1,700 journals through the AVU digital library, and this number is destined to grow to over 2,400 journals. In the world today and more so in the 21st century, development is and will become increasingly dominated by the new forces of modern technology. Universities must participate and benefit from the emerging science and technological revolution. Unless African universities take up the challenge, they face the prospect of becoming marginalized.

Research and Development
Research is one of the principal missions of the university. From the early 1960s, research was viewed as a tool for teaching and was mainly undertaken by foreign professors. In the 1970s and 1980s, the volume of research from universities grew steadily and was increasingly being undertaken by African scholars. In addition, a steady build-up of research capacity was achieved by most African universities in the 1970s. In Kenya, for example, units dealing with research were established within universities—such as the Bureau of Educational Research at Kenyatta University and the Institute of Development Studies at Nairobi University. However, in the 1990s, research at African universities

started to decline due to lack of funds, among other reasons. Decline in institutional research reduces the ability of universities to acquire and use new knowledge and play an authoritative leadership role with respect to policy issues in various sectors of development. In the 21st century, African universities must put more emphasis on research and make a deliberate effort to facilitate training, engage in research, and disseminate findings. This will help build the much-needed intellectual capacity in research.

University Education and Unemployment
The population explosion, expansion of student enrollments, the types of degree programs offered, and the poor economic situation in most African countries have all contributed to high levels of unemployment among university graduates. In most universities in Africa, university graduates in the arts and humanities are in oversupply, while other professions are undersupplied. Universities in Africa must ensure that their degree programs have the potential to get graduates employed. Universities must also prepare students to respond to growing opportunities for self-employment. This requires reviewing the programs and methods of teaching and making them responsive to market demands. In Kenya, most universities are attacking the unemployment problem by introducing such programs. Students are also encouraged to equip themselves with the necessary skills (e.g., with computers) to make themselves more versatile.

Another strategy for tackling the unemployment problem is to intensify the links between the university and the private sector. Few universities in Africa have taken the initiative to establish such links. Most of the training provided is thus not based on the needs of industry. Links and partnerships with the private sector can provide opportunities for employment and hence participation in economic development.

Conclusion
Innovative thinking and new strategies are essential guides to future educational provision and practice. Such strategies include improvement of evaluation and accreditation systems, review of programs to make them more responsive to societal needs, informed management of higher education, enhancement of gender equity, promotion of university linkages with the private sector, and involvement in policy analysis through research. In addition, improvement of higher education will require more effective utilization of new information and communica-

tion technologies. Universities in Africa need to review their missions and come up with specific strategic plans for the 21st century, based on each university's unique situation, as well as national and global issues affecting universities.

Reference

Ishumi, Abel. 1994. *Thirty years of learning: International development research centre.* Ottawa, Canada.

5.
South Africa:
FUTURE PROSPECTS

NASIMA BADSHA

South African higher education is in the process of major transformation. A policy framework (*Education White Paper: A Programme for the Transformation of Higher Education*) was adopted in mid-1997, after an extensive process of investigation and consultation that included a National Commission on Higher Education. A new higher education act was also promulgated in late 1997. While the changes to South African higher education were precipitated by the end of apartheid, the issues and conditions that shape its transformation are not dissimilar to those that impact systems elsewhere in the world. The *Education White Paper* states that policy must promote:

•   *Increased and broadened participation.* This is seen as central to overcoming historically determined inequalities in the system. Increased access for blacks and women and for disabled and mature students and the development of new curricula and flexible models of teaching and learning, to accommodate a larger and more diverse student body, are identified as key policy objectives.

•   *Responsiveness to societal interests and needs.* Higher education must be restructured to meet the needs of an increasingly technologically oriented economy; to deliver the requisite research, highly trained people, and knowledge to equip a developing society with the capacity to address national needs; and to participate in a rapidly changing and competitive global context.

- *Cooperation and partnerships in governance.* This requires the reconceptualization of the relationship between higher education and the state, civil society, and stakeholders, and among institutions (*Education White Paper* 1997, 10).

In essence, the higher education system is required to redress past inequalities as well as to meet the development needs of society, in a rapidly changing global context. It is required to do so in a climate of relative fiscal austerity, and a funding environment that places greater emphasis on accountability for the expenditure of public funds, market principles, and efficiency and effectiveness.

The policy and legislative framework is in place, but the challenges of implementation are only beginning to impact on the system. Policy implementation is made all the more difficult in a system that remains uneven. South African higher education currently comprises 21 universities and 15 technikons, which are higher education institutions that largely concentrate on career-oriented and vocational education. These institutions have different histories and capacities, largely shaped by the country's apartheid legacy. The universities and technikons continue to be divided along lines of historically black and white institutions. Research and graduate education is largely concentrated at the historically white institutions. However, in terms of student enrollments, demographic patterns have changed significantly over the past decade. Historically black institutions, have, in the main, concentrated on undergraduate education, with the large percentage of enrollments being in the arts, humanities, education, and social sciences. Central to the transformation agenda for South African higher education, as spelled out in the *Education White Paper*, is the goal of conceptualizing, planning, governing, and funding higher education as a single coordinated system. The focus is on developing an integrated and coordinated system, rather than a uniform one. The need for diversity in the system, especially in relation to the institutional forms, has been acknowledged to be essential if a larger and more diverse student body is to be accommodated.

Planning and Funding
New planning and funding mechanisms have been identified as the key policy instruments for achieving the primary policy goals. The planning framework revolves around two key instruments: the development of a national higher education plan and institutional three-year rolling

plans. For the first time in the history of higher education in the country, all universities and technikons were required by government to produce three-year rolling plans that, in this pilot planning year, focused on four policy areas: size and shape of program offerings and projected student enrollments; staff and student equity; efficiency measures; and interinstitutional cooperation.

These plans will contribute to the phased development of a broad national plan, which is intended to articulate targets for the size and shape of the system, overall growth and participation rates, and institutional and program mixes. In future, the approval of institutional plans will determine funding for higher education institutions. The requirement to develop institutional plans has provided the impetus for institutions to fundamentally reassess their missions and capacities.

New funding arrangements are currently being developed and will comprise two elements: formula-based operating grants, primarily for teaching and related recurrent costs, and payable on the basis of approved enrollments in different fields and levels of study as related to the institutional plans; and earmarked funds for specific purposes such as research development and capital works. In 1998, earmarked funding was allocated for institutional redress, targeted to building capacity at the historically disadvantaged institutions in areas such as libraries and information technology.

The funding of higher education is also based on a sharing of costs between private beneficiaries and the state. However, given that many students from poor families do not have the capacity to pay, a National Student Financial Aid Scheme (NSFAS) has been established to provide for bursary and loan funding for academically able students from economically disadvantaged backgrounds. The scheme is dependent on annual budgetary allocations from the state and on income generated from loan repayments. There has been considerable interest in linking student financial aid to community service, but this possibility requires thorough investigation, especially in relation to the cost implications.

Since 1994, over R1.2 billion has been contributed to the NSFAS, largely by the South African government but with some international donor funding. The NSFAS, like similar schemes elsewhere in the world, is not able to meet the full demand for student financial assistance. To date, there has of most been relatively little private-sector interest in augmenting the scheme.

It is anticipated that the consolidation of the NSFAS will, in the coming years, be central to supporting the broadening of student access. However, many institutions continue to face the consequences of student fee debt, both historic and current, which places an additional burden on the budgets of public higher education institutions.

Curriculum Transformation
At an institutional level, considerable change is taking place in relationship to the curriculum, and this is being shaped, in part, by the development of a national qualifications framework (NQF), which spans the entire education and training system. The NQF is aimed at improving human resources development by promoting greater coherence between education and training and improving access to, and progression through, recognized qualifications for learners at all levels. Despite initial resistance on the part of higher education to participation in the NQF, all higher education qualifications are currently in the process of being registered on the NQF. The criticisms of the NQF are based on a number of concerns, such as fears of a drift toward vocationalism, undesirable standardization, and an overemphasis on outcomes—all of which are perceived as being antithetical to the ethos of higher education. The NQF and related quality assurance mechanisms have nevertheless prompted the development of higher education programs that are more responsive to the world of work and that enjoy greater coherence and attention to core academic skills. There is also a growing debate on the Africanization of the curriculum and its implications for teaching and research.

Student Access
Some of the complexities of the transformation of South African higher education can be highlighted by focusing on access and related issues of equity. The total number of African students in higher education increased by an annual average of 14 percent between 1986 and 1993, as against 0.4 percent for white South Africans. The overall participation rate of about 20 percent in 1993 continues to be characterized by inequalities—the participation rate for white students being just under 70 percent, while that for African students was about 12 percent (*Education White Paper* 1997, 20). Since 1993, these disparities have diminished, and African students now comprise the majority of students

enrolled at universities and technikons. Women students now make up approximately 55 percent of the overall student enrollment. These figures, while indicative of enrollment trends, mask significant disparities in the enrollment of black and women students in both graduate studies and in certain fields, such as science, engineering, and technology.

In the past few years, growth in the system has not been sustained at anticipated levels. A number of factors account for this, including the unfavorable economic climate and poor completion rate for qualified black students from the school system (especially for entry into science, engineering, and technology fields). White student numbers are on the decline within the public higher education sector, with increasing numbers enrolling in the growing number of private higher education institutions. Within the public sector, significant shifts in student enrollment patterns are occurring, with increasing numbers of black students entering the historically white institutions. These trends are less marked in the technikons, which continue to attract students into more vocationally oriented programs. The historically black universities are, in particular, facing declining student numbers. Although this does offer the opportunity for these institutions to consolidate the significant expansion that was experienced by many of them in the early 1990s, it does precipitate the need for higher education institutions to become more responsive to changing needs, especially in relation to the world of work.

The current situation does also allow the system the opportunity to plan for growth levels that are both affordable and in line with the social and economic needs of the country. Hopefully, steps can be taken to avoid the negative consequences (such as overcrowded facilities, poor-quality programs, and low research output and quality) of unplanned growth without the injection of extra resources.

Increasing numbers of students from elsewhere in Africa are enrolling at South African higher education institutions, with the greatest number coming from the southern African region. Students from southern African countries are treated as "home students," with respect to the payment of fees. Similarly, all foreign graduate students are subsidized by government to the same extent as local students, as a way of promoting the internationalization of South African higher education at the graduate level. Particular attention is being paid to the role of South Africa in building high-level human resources capacity in Africa. Similarly, the development of research partnerships between South African universities and technikons and their counterparts elsewhere on the continent is high on the agenda. There is concern that such relationships be firmly based on principles of mutual cooperation and partnership.

Staff Access and Development
The profile of staff at higher education institutions remains largely colored by the apartheid legacy. It is often said that "the greater the prestige, status and influence particular positions have, the more they are dominated by white staff members and men. Positions with lower status, prestige, and influence tend to be dominated primarily by black staff members and women" (National Commission on Higher Education 1996, 141). It is becoming increasingly evident that one of the most difficult challenges facing South African higher education is to change the race and gender profile of its staff, particularly in the senior academic and management echelons. Currently, institutions face considerable difficulty in recruiting and retaining the relatively small pool of qualified black staff—for a range of reasons, but particularly because higher education salaries are lagging behind those of the private sector and the civil service. Besides the need to address the conditions of service for staff in higher education, there is considerable emphasis on "growing our own timber," through a range of graduate and staff development programs.

The *Education White Paper* emphasises that the successful development of a single coordinated system requires more than a commitment to transformation. It is critically dependent on building and enhancing capacity in all spheres—academic, management, governance, and infrastructural—to give effect to new policies and to ensure efficient functioning. The White Paper identifies a number of areas for particular attention—such as management, leadership, and strategic planning and the provision of administrative and infrastructural support for teaching and research.

Private Higher Education
There is a relatively established private higher education sector in South Africa, offering programs largely through franchise agreements with local and international universities but also under the institutions' own auspices. The programs offered are largely limited to fields such as business administration, communications, and information technology.

44

The role that the growing private higher education sector will play to shape access patterns in the coming years is unclear. The 1997 Higher Education Act provides for the registration of private higher education institutions and is aimed at protecting the public from "fly-by-night" operations that have mushroomed over the past few years.

The criteria for registration of private higher education institutions include an assessment of the financial viability of the institution and the quality of its academic programs, which must not be "inferior to standards at a comparable public higher education institution" (Higher Education Act 1997, 34). Foreign universities operating in South Africa, either directly or via local partners, will undoubtedly influence the higher education landscape. However, their commitment to equity, relevance, and quality remains to be seen.

Conclusion
Only some of the issues explored in the theme chapter have been discussed from a South African perspective. However, all are of relevance to the South African context, and each could be refracted through our experiences and through different lenses (i.e., that of government, higher education institutions, academics, students, etc.). Especially given the wide-ranging and ambitious transformation agenda that we have embarked on, the opportunity to be a part of in-depth discussion of the key issues facing higher education worldwide is timely and welcome.

References
Education White Paper 3-A: Programme for the transformation of higher education. 1997. Pretoria: Department of Education.
Higher Education Act No. 101. 1997.
National Commission on Higher Education. 1996. *A framework for transformation*.

6.

Latin America:
NATIONAL RESPONSES TO WORLD CHALLENGES IN HIGHER EDUCATION

SIMON SCHWARTZMAN

"Globalization," the buzzword of the third millennium, is nothing new for Latin American universities. The first academic institutions in the region were established in the 16th century by the Catholic Church. The national states created after the independence movements of the early 19th century tried to copy the then modern, technically oriented French educational institutions. In recent decades, American research universities and graduate schools became the model to follow. Today, however, the old pattern of adoption and copy of foreign models has become just a small part of a much broader trend of international integration, which has as one of its consequences a series of features, problems, and concerns that affect most higher educational systems in similar ways, while eliciting different and often contradictory responses.

Mass Higher Education

In Latin America as elsewhere, mass higher education developed in the 1960s and in later years not as purposeful projects of governments and university administrators, but as a consequence of large-scale social, economic, and cultural changes beyond anyone's control.[1] In different ways in different countries, a combination of forces were driving the enormous increase in demand for higher education: the concentration of populations in large cities; the entrance of women into the labor market; the gradual expansion of basic and secondary education; the development of the youth culture; the movement of adults to acquire new qualifications, certifications, and job opportunities; the new skills required by modern industry and services; and the expansion of the welfare state and public services. As of 1990, the higher education enrollments had reached a gross rate of 40 percent in Argentina, 33 percent in Peru, 26 percent in Costa Rica, and 20 percent in Cuba. In these countries and in others like Mexico (with an enrollment rate of 14 percent), the public, national universities opened their doors to almost everybody who could apply, becoming among the largest higher education institutions in the world. In other places, like Brazil, Colombia, and Chile, the public and more traditional universities resisted the onslaught, trying to maintain their traditions and areas of competence. A new tier of higher education institutions developed, mostly as private endeavors, sometimes at the provincial and local levels. Their enrollment rates did not grow as much—11 percent in Brazil, 14.2 percent in Colombia, and 20.6 percent in Chile. These figures are also a reflection of the relative size of the urban centers and the new middle classes in each country. Mixed situations occur everywhere. Elite institutions have opened courses in more popular subjects for less-qualified students; open-admission universities created and maintained niches of competence and excellence; and a small, well-endowed group of private institutions emerged to cater to the children of the elites.

Institutional Change and Differentiation

The need to accommodate an increasingly large number of students in a traditional university setting is just the most obvious aspect of a much deeper problem, which is how to adapt traditional institutions to a completely new set of social groups, functions, and demands. In spite of the cultural traditions coming from the Iberian peninsula, and the growing economic presence of Britain in Latin America since the years of independence, it is to France that Latin American politicians and intellectuals looked for the institutional models for their new states, including their institutions of higher learning. Many explanations could be given for this fact: Anglo-Saxon culture and traditions were more alien, and their language more remote. More to the point, perhaps, were the revolutionary rhetoric and France's effort to build a modern nation through the strength of the state, an appealing model when civil society was so weak and the economy so poorly developed as in Latin America.

The new, public higher education institutions were to train the lawyers, engineers, military officers, and medical doctors to build the new nations, and the students in these institutions did not expect any less from their careers. General education was to be provided in the early period to the selected few, usually by the Church, and vocational and practical training for the masses was to occur on the job, if ever. Higher education was reserved for the new professions, and the new graduates were to become the intelligentsia of their societies. This explains the long tradition of student politics in Latin America, as well as the universities' usual disregard for scientific scholarship and technical expertise, with the usual and notable exceptions.

This arrangement is now being challenged from all sides. From the bottom, large numbers of applicants are hoping to get the same access to prestigious positions and income as the old elites, but willing to settle for recognized skills and a valid credential in the labor market. From the top, a new, small but vocal generation of foreign-trained academics and international advisers is calling for scientific research and advanced technical prowess, without which modernization and economic development will not materialize. And, from all sides, new ways of doing politics and gaining power are emerging, not respecting the status credentials of the old elite, and a competitive market in which traditional academic and family entitlements did not count as in the past.

The old universities had to change, and in fact have been doing so in recent decades, even if erratically most of the time. Countries that had kept their public universities protected allowed a new tier of higher education institutions to develop, copying as well as they could the established models, but offering evening classes, not requiring much in terms of performance, and charging students what they could pay. Countries that opted for open access to all students got used to enormous rates of student retention and dropouts in the first years, and all developed "graduate" programs to enhance the selection of their elites, and to answer the demands for research and scholarship.

Graduate Education and Research
To preserve, and even to enhance, the old centers of quality and ex-

cellence was probably the easy part, although not without its problems. It is always easier, and much cheaper, to take care of a selected group of students and their teachers than to change large higher education systems as a whole, or to adapt them to an extended and highly differentiated set of new clients.

It is not by chance that what is "graduate" in the United States is called "postgraduate" in Latin America and Europe, and what is "graduate" in these regions is called "undergraduate" in the United States. Undergraduate, college education, as conceived in the United States and the United Kingdom, was always understood as part of secondary education on the European continent and in Latin America. "Postgraduate" education was never situated in specialized institutions, course programs, and "graduate schools," which are recognized as an American invention. Brazil is probably the one country in Latin America that went further in the introduction of American-style graduate programs in their universities, which were duly rechristened as "postgraduate," and placed in the country's best public institutions.

These programs perform at least three functions. The first is the stated one—to provide a place for education in advanced research and scholarship. There are several, good-quality programs of this kind, especially at some of the federal universities (in Rio de Janeiro and Minas Gerais) and mostly at the public universities supported by the São Paulo state (the Universities of São Paulo and Campinas). They employ most of the active researchers in Brazil, in all fields. The second is to provide credentials and continuing education to academic personnel in public universities. In Brazil, as in a number of other countries, new standards required credentials of academics that they did not possess. The countries could not provide enough personnel who met the new standards. The intentions were good, but the consequences were often problematic. In Brazil, graduate programs have mushroomed into the hundreds since the 1970s, most of them providing master's and "specialist" degrees that were accepted as second-best. Still, today only 16 percent of academic faculty in Brazil hold a doctoral degree—concentrated in a few places, such as the universities in the State of São Paulo—compared with 25 percent with M.A.s, 36 percent with some kind of specialist degree, and 22 percent with just an undergraduate diploma. The third function of the new graduate programs is to provide advanced skills and enhanced credentials for some students in an enlarged market. For the lawyers, economists, engineers, administrators, medical doctors, and others who pursue higher degrees with that purpose in mind, the research requirements of the graduate programs are a nuisance, and they often drop out of the programs and forget about their academic commitments when their job situation improves. A final and very important reason to get into graduate education is to postpone entry into the labor market. In Brazil this phenomenon has helped by the existence of an extensive system of student fellowships for a significant portion of graduate students.

To control the quality of graduate education, the Brazilian Ministry of Education maintains an elaborate and well-reputed system of peer review evaluation of these programs. Data for the 1996/1997 period show the existence of 1,293 programs, half of them providing doctoral degrees. In an evaluation scale from one to seven, in which six means high quality, and seven corresponds to international quality standards, 83.1 percent received between three and five, 9.5 percent got six or seven, and 7.4 percent flunked with less than three points.

Undergraduate Education

The combination of growing enrollments and the import of the U.S. model of graduate education transformed and downgraded large sections of the existing graduate higher education system in Latin America to a kind of undergraduate level. This was seldom done on purpose, although the 1968 university reform in Brazil did create something called "basic courses," which were to last for one or two years as a preparation for professional degrees and which failed almost everywhere. With the expanding youth culture, most 18-year-old students do not know how to choose a profession. Yet the notion that they should work on their general skills for some years after secondary school is very alien to the Latin American tradition, in spite of the absence of anything similar to European standards of good-quality, college-like secondary education.

In addition to general education, undergraduate programs need to provide vocational training, teacher education, and continuous, lifelong education. Eighteen-year-olds coming straight from acceptable secondary schools and aiming at long-term university degree programs are a minority within the larger student population comprised of older students, returning students, those that are in midcareer, and those who lack the necessary training to enter an academic-level program. In practice, a large portion of the new demand for higher education was in the form of evening classes and four-year programs in fields such as administration, economics, accounting, and law, which seldom led to actual professional standing (only a small percentage of the students with law degrees in Brazil actually apply for and pass the bar examinations). Rather, these programs provide a credential their graduates can show when hunting for jobs, and at best some basic and general knowledge and skills that may be of practical value to graduates. A special case is the training of teachers in basic and secondary education—careers that are low-prestige and low-paying and usually embraced only in the absence of other opportunities.

Modern, mass higher education systems should be able to differentiate among these groups and their demands and provide each with the training necessary and compatible with their skills, aspirations, and needs. Very little of that is being done in Latin America, and it is probably unrealistic to expect such a vast undertaking from the central bureaucracies—which are still in place in most countries in the region—as they try to steer their higher education systems in some direction.

Finance
The most that governments can do is to manage the limited resources they have, given the mounting costs of higher education, in a context of increasing competition over public funds and the stark need to balance public budgets. The growth of public expenditures in higher education, which took place almost everywhere, was not just a consequence of expanding enrollments. The old faculties had been staffed by lawyers, medical doctors, and engineers who earned most of their incomes from their work as professionals. The rising expenditures went to pay the salaries of the large numbers of full-time academic and nonacademic employees staffing the new institutions. In public universities, these academic and nonacademic employees often receive the benefits of civil servants and are protected from firing, with assured promotion based on seniority and generous retirement benefits. These high costs, when combined with academic selectivity and inefficiencies in the allocation of resources, can lead to very high per capita expenditures. In 1990, Brazil spent about U.S.$9,000 per year, per student in federal institutions; compared with about U.S.$1,500 for Chile, Costa Rica, and Venezuela; around U.S.$1,000 for Argentina, Colombia, Honduras, Mexico, and Uruguay; and around U.S.$500 or less for Bolivia, Cuba, Ecuador, Haiti, Nicaragua, Paraguay, and Peru. These figures are imprecise, since there is no clear definition of a "student,"

and the costs may include things like retirement benefits and teaching hospitals. The figures may in some cases reflect the laws and benefits relating to public employees rather than the quality of higher education provided by each country.

But public expenditure is just one part of the story. The estimation for 1998 was that Brazil would spend about U.S.$14 billion a year on higher education, U.S.$6 billion coming from the central government for the 350,000 students in federal universities, U.S.$5 billion from state governments for the 250,000 students in state institutions, and about U.S.$3 billion in tuition paid by the approximately 1.2 million students in private institutions. Brazil obviously needs to raise higher education enrollments to levels similar to those in other countries in the region and in the world, but it is unlikely that much higher levels of public support will be forthcoming. Other Latin American countries are also unlikely to increase their expenditures to anything similar to Brazil's per capita levels in the near future.

The possible alternatives are to use public resources more efficiently, bringing in more students without increasing funding; to expand the share of the private sector in the financing of higher education, charging tuition in public institutions (which is done in countries like Chile and some parts of Argentina, for instance, but is still taboo in Brazil); and to increase the cost of tuition everywhere. Tuition costs may reduce demand but may create social inequities, which have to be compensated by needs-based fellowships and student loans. The problems of financing higher education in Latin America are not only a matter of limited resources but, in large part, a question of how to better use what is already there.

Institutional Reform
To make better use of money, and to provide the students with what they expect, deep institutional reforms are necessary. Most governments in the region have tried them, always encountering strong resistance, and with different degrees of success. There is a growing consensus on what has to be done. Public money for public universities has to be given according to clear criteria of performance and products delivered, not just according to historical trends or political influence. More broadly, a system of coordination based on the bureaucratic authority of the state needs to give way to one based more on competitive markets—not just markets of buyers and sellers of educational

products in the private sector, but of providers and users of good-quality academic and educational products. In the ideological disputes that surround higher education reform, this plea for more market-based, instead of bureaucratic regulation, is often derided as "privatization." However, the public sector can and probably will remain a key provider of funds for higher education; its way of acting will have to change, from bureaucratic management to the creation of mechanisms to promote competition in quality and performance among institutions.

The third corner of Burton Clark's well-known "coordination triangle," besides government and market, namely oligarchy, also has a role to play in the new context. The cosy arrangements, by which prestigious professors and academics used to make most of the decisions related to their work without explanation, cannot be maintained once systems get so complex and differentiated, with many conflicting goals and interests. Diffuse notions of prestige, competence, and quality have to be replaced, or at least complemented by more precise information stemming from well-conceived tests, performance measures, and statistical analysis. Still, academic and professional authority will always be needed. Evaluation and accreditation committees are being established everywhere, creating rankings, allocating resources, and evaluating new and existing programs. Prestigious scholars and professors are the only ones with the legitimacy to establish the rules of the new "academic markets," and to act as counterweights to the bureaucratic and centralizing tendencies of governments.

Reforms at the coordination level have to be followed by changes at the institutional level. The decisions to be made by university administrators in this new context of intense competition, complex tasks, and scarce resources are very different and much more difficult than those of the past, when the only things to be decided were who should teach what in each semester, and who would participate in the various academic commissions. Most public higher education institutions in Latin America, however, still function as in the old days, with decisions taken after lengthy faculty meetings, and without help from professional administrators and staff. The new context requires more power and authority for the central administration, external supervision, and a better system of making difficult decisions on personnel, academic programs, and enrollment policies. There is still a long way to go in this direction, especially in public institutions, given the need to change rules related to the civil service, and also to alter the relative power of different groups within the institutions.

The New Challenges

The issues outlined above—regarding mass higher education, undergraduate and graduate education, financing and institutional reform—have been on the higher education agenda in Latin America for many years, and are far from being resolved in most places. The main reason for this slow pace is the high political costs of reform. Students, academics, and administrators do not know much about the complexities of change in higher education, and often have good reason to mistrust their governments. Moreover, they feel they might be directly affected by reforms leading to closer evaluation of what a lecturer does in class, or whether a student is really learning, or whether money is being spent wisely. Many sectors in society would favor these reforms: employers hoping for more-qualified employees, families looking for good schools for their children, less-privileged persons looking for more suitable learning opportunities, governments needing to cut spending or to make better use of their resources. But these potential supporters of change are scattered, while the stakeholders within higher education institutions are well organized, able to demonstrate against the government, and have easy access to the press. No wonder that some of the biggest transformations in higher education in Latin America were accomplished by authoritarian regimes. However, to thrive, higher education institutions require personal involvement and legitimacy, which are characteristics of free and democratic societies. In Chile and Brazil, democratic regimes tried to build on what military governments had left in terms of effective institutional improvements, while getting rid of the authoritarian components of the previous years.

While reform is likely to be slow and erratic, there are new challenges that can increase the pace of change. The most important is probably the fact that Latin American universities are gradually losing their monopoly on granting diplomas and professional credentials. Until recently, Uruguay had just one university, and the idea that private institutions could compete with it was inconceivable. Today, other institutions are emerging, and the Universidad de la República is feeling the pressure of competition. In Argentina and Mexico, provincial universities were slow to appear, and were always looked upon with mistrust by the large national universities in Buenos Aires and Mexico City. Even in Brazil, with a large private sector and strong Catholic universities, the private sector is still widely mistrusted, and the government holds the right to decide who can and cannot teach, what is to be taught (albeit in very general terms), and whether specific academic programs meet the standards defined by the ministerial authorities. This supervisory power is justified by the need to control the quality of teaching and protect the students and the public—but with the side effect of restricting competition in the more regulated sectors of the job market and of stifling creativity and innovation.

What remains of this monopolistic or quasimonopolistic power seems to be eroding very rapidly. The job market is reducing its reliance on educational credentials, and requiring more competence and skills, which can be provided not only by formal educational institutions and formal programs, but also by a host of new entrepreneurs, who are discovering the new possibilities of the "education industry." Educational institutions in the United Kingdom, the United States, and other countries are starting to establish alliances, partnerships, and franchises in different parts of the world, including Latin America. Distance learning is still in its infancy but has the potential to wreak havoc with national and regional barriers. The international mobility of students, which until recently had been limited to graduate students, is providing an alternative to the increasing costs of domestic private education for undergraduates in higher income brackets.

In this scenario, institutions that depend upon a steady flow of public money, uncomplaining students, and a monopolistic hold on the education market are bound to disappear or deteriorate, losing their best professional staff and academic faculty. Latin American higher education institutions are finally becoming aware of this new situation and starting to adjust to it, rather than merely waiting for broader systemwide changes. Because of this, there are good reasons for hope.

Note
1. For an overview of Latin American higher education and its policy agenda, see José Joaquin Brunner, coordinator, and Jorge Balán, et al., Educación superior en América Latina: Una agenda para el año 2000, Proyecto de políticas comparadas de educación superior (Bogotá, Universidad nacional de Colombia, 1995); see also the special issue of Higher Education, 25, 1, 1993, on Latin America, ed. José Joaquin

Brunner and Simon Schwartzman; and Simon Schwartzman, América Latina: Universidades en transición (Washington, D.C.: Organization of American States, 1996).

7.

Universal Problems and National Realities:
JAPAN IN COMPARATIVE PERSPECTIVE

AKIMASA MITSUTA

"Academic institutions worldwide stem from common historical roots and face common contemporary challenges," according to the theme chapter in this book. Probably many people involved in higher education in Japan would fully agree with this opinion, and it is echoed in official government statements. The authors' view that certain issues are "central to current development in higher education worldwide" would probably be shared by many Japanese academic policymakers as well. However, in my view, the real problems facing Japanese higher education stem from a long history and tradition not shared by the Western academy. The serious problems Japanese society and education confront are uniquely Japanese, and can be solved only by the Japanese themselves. Thus the issues raised by the theme chapter may superficially look similar worldwide, but the reasons they occur in Japan may be quite different from the reasons they occur in Western countries. It is necessary to see whether they sprout from the same root and whether the implications are the same in other nations.

In my view, identifying the historical factors that produced these differences will provide more ideas for solving problems that appear to be universal. To understand the differences, historical understanding is definitely needed, as is socioeconomic analysis—even though the issues concern education. They are universal issues but truly national problems.

General Historical Background

The issues described in the theme chapter are all perfectly legitimate with reference to universities within the Western hemisphere, or systems created as a result of European colonization. However, in a country like Japan, which encountered Western powers less than 200 years ago, many issues must be interpreted differently. Much more attention should be paid to the fact that before the 2 centuries of interaction with the West, Japan had a history of 200 centuries. This fact influences not only Japan's approach to matters of higher education but also to all other issues facing the country. While Japan's problems may appear similar to those confronting America and Europe, fundamentally Japanese do not share the same traditions or perspectives as those produced by Western civilization. Seeming similar but being different is the key to understanding and addressing the questions in Japan. What makes the situation worse in recent years is that many individuals in Japan fail to understand or study their own history, leading to a lack of awareness of the real problems.

Japan started to modernize only in the mid-19th century. Although this process was called "modernization," it was really "learning from the West." The reason Japan sought to do this is an ironic one: in order to maintain its independence from Western colonial powers, Japan had to accept and adapt notions of Western civilization. The nation tried to learn from the Western powers that were endangering its independence and traditions. Tokyo Imperial University was established anew following the European model—but not in order to turn the society into a miniature European country. A phrase in use until the end of World War II, "Wa-kon Yo-sai," captured this approach well; it can be translated as "strengthening the Japanese spirit by using Western technologies."

In forming the imperial university after a European model, the Japanese government did not officially abandon the historical roots of the institution going back to a school named Shoheiko, during the Edo Period, before modernization. Tokyo Imperial University had strong departments of Chinese philosophy and literature and national (Japanese) history and literature. The university had an engineering school, something not common in Western universities at the time but reflecting the traditional value placed on technical training by the Japanese. These various elements demonstrate that the Japanese modeled their university system on Western institutions but did not simply imitate German or British universities.

The effort not to be submerged into and overwhelmed by Western civilization has led to the current push toward internationalization by Japanese universities and Japanese enterprises.

A Common Language

The theme chapter indicates that "academic institutions have frequently been international in orientation—with common curricular elements and, in the medieval period, a common language of instruction, Latin." Early in Japan's opening to the West, Japanese scholars went to Europe and America to study, returning home with many books written in European languages. These books were then assigned to their students, but the basic language of instruction remained Japanese. For a short period, Tokyo Imperial University employed many foreign scholars who taught in European languages. However, the bulk of teaching in Japanese universities has been in the Japanese language from the very beginning. There is one well-known episode, in which a minister of education (Arinori Mori) who had studied in the United States proposed making English the language of instruction for all Japanese education, but his proposal was not supported by the public at large and was not adopted.

As the theme chapter says, "at the end of the 20th century, English has assumed a role as the primary international language of science and scholarship, including the Internet." As English-language dominance spreads, the more resistance there will be from nations such as Japan and France that are not willing to consider English as their national language. On this matter, it is important to examine the differences between universities in former colonial states and those in Japan, China, and Thailand, which were basically never colonized. Today, even though English seems to be the international language, especially in science, it is not the language of instruction in universities in Japan, Korea, Thailand, or China, although it is in Singapore and other countries colonized by Great Britain.

The impact of this basic difference cannot be overlooked. The role of universities in Japan was to absorb the fruits of scientific activities and to integrate them into the national language and culture. The first generation translated all the scientific and technical works published in Europe and America into Japanese and proceeded to conduct its own research and scholarship in Japanese. This fundamental pattern has not changed even though at present many scholars can conduct their research and publish their papers in English.

In terms of the Internet, accessing the system and the flood of information on it does require the use of English. However, it should be noted that in Japan and in China much effort is being devoted to how to transform the system and translate its contents from English into Japanese and Chinese, respectively. This effort may appear a waste of time and energy, but if the question is whether or not to accept English as the national language, the answer is very clear for the countries whose academic roots are deep in non-European soil.

While the short-term goal, to promote the study of English, may be a legitimate one, the nation must still wrestle with the more serious question of how to maintain its national identity. For instance, in Japan a debate has been ongoing over whether to begin teaching English in primary school. In the most recent discussions on this issue in the Central Council of Education, the conclusion was not to do so.

Moving from Elite, to Mass, to Universal Access
This appears to be the trend in Japan as it is in many Western countries. However, this is a trend that has existed for over one thousand years in Japan. At the time of the Meiji Restoration, during the period of modernization in the 19th century, the literacy rate was already over 50 percent. Japan has historically been an essentially classless society. The masses were always in a position to share a stake in the most advanced culture. People may say that the imperial universities were not for the masses. In terms of enrollment ratios, this argument is legitimate. However, more importantly, since the mid-19th century, the mission of the modern educational system in Japan has been commonly understood to develop the potential of people all over the country, not restricted to a certain group of people. Unlike in the British tradition, in Japan the chance for higher education existed for even the poorest family. The imperial universities were not for an elite class but rather functioned to cultivate elites. In a sense, mass higher education has always existed, and an elite education system has never existed.

The policy issue in Japan is not how to expand education to the masses. The serious question is whether or not a public effort can be made to preserve elite education in a homogeneous nation such as Japan.

Financial Constraints

Another worldwide issue—higher education funding—is likewise one that can only be completely understood when it is seen as a national issue instead of as a worldwide phenomenon. Generally speaking, the increased population share heading toward higher education definitely requires increased funding. In Japan, the enrollment rate in universities has already reached approximately 40 percent of the college-age population. There are about 600 universities in Japan. Of them, 98 are "national" universities, operated with funding from the national budget. The Ministry of Education, Science, Culture, and Sports controls about 10 percent of the national budget. Of the ministry's total budget, about one quarter goes to support the national universities, including 16 independent research institutions. The ministry also provides some subsidy to a number of private universities. But it can be said that the national institutions are the core of higher education and most advanced research.

Therefore, the shortage of funding for higher education turns into the problem of whether the national budget allocation is sufficient. Generally speaking, historically, the percentage received by each sector in the national budget can hardly be changed. Thus to the public at large the financial issue involves the size of the national budget, and those involved in higher education must ask whether special consideration can be paid to higher education within the national budget. In America the issue would be where to find the resources and who should bear the cost. Many other sources of funding are generated in the United States to fund higher education and research. But in Japan, learning Western science has from the beginning been understood as a national mission rather than an individual one. The common understanding among the Japanese people remains that the Ministry of Education, Science, Culture, and Sports is the appropriate agency to provide support for this sector within the national budget. While much is said about diversifying funding sources, not many people really believe that the private sector should bear the cost for education and research.

The financial constraints and the increase in the percentage of the population receiving higher education have led to a significant move by the Ministry of Education. There has been concern that Japanese basic research may not be competitive with that in other advanced nations. How can Japan catch up with the West, given that it began its scientific research 200 years later than the West? In 1996, the Japanese government announced a "basic plan on science and technology," with an aim to double its investment in research and development during the next five years. For 1999, the government has announced a planned increase in the total size of the national budget by issuing national bonds. This will ease the constraints on the education budget as well.

As a foreigner observing the United States, the situation appears quite different. There, research universities that are members of the Association of American Universities are less influenced by shifts in federal funding policy, since their leading role is recognized not only by the national government but by industry and by the entire world. Richard Atkinson, president of the University of California system, stated, in a speech given in Tokyo in November 1997, "I am more optimistic than many of my colleagues that the federal government will find a way to continue funding university research at a reasonable level." It seems the major concern of higher education in the United States is how to deal with the masses seeking higher education and the quality of education provided to the increasing population at the tertiary level, while in Japan the major concern is how to promote basic research.

Education and Work
The relationship between education and work is crucial everywhere. However, the nature of the concern may be quite different from country to country. To understand the situation, one has to consider the employment system after industrialization, since the last century, and the tradition of human relations—including family ties. In these small matters, social practices differ quite a bit from those in the United States. Therefore, while it is superficially possible to discuss as a worldwide issue, substantively the core of the problem is different.

The theme chapter says "professional education often links well to employment in many countries, but education in the arts and sciences is less well articulated." In a society like Japan's, the question is whether the workplace expects any professional training to take place in the school system itself. Within the Confucian tradition, education has long been considered as a process of cultivating character. Comparable ideas may be a "liberal education" in America and a "gentleman's education" in Britain.

This feeling and the paternalistic climate of Japanese society have led to the practice that not much professional training is expected by industries when they employ new graduates. Dramatic socioeconomic changes are now occurring in Japan. Some observers say the lifetime employment system has already collapsed. If so, the substance of education given in schools and colleges may truly become an issue. However, during the recruitment of new graduates in 1998, most employers and applicants still believed in the notion of lifetime employment. That belief means it is less important whether one has studied a specific subject in school and acquired certain skills than whether the new employee will be a loyal member of the organization. Professional training will come after that within the organization.

The notion of lifetime employment, whether or not it continues as a reality, is the key to understanding various issues concerning education or social matters in Japan. Since not many countries have this system, most educational issues in Japan are not universal ones. In the United States, the question is how better to link education or training in schools and colleges to the workplace. In Japan, the question is whether schools or colleges should be useful in terms of professional job training.

Internationalization
In today's Japan, the most crucial issue in higher education is internationalization. The concept is not well defined, but everyone involved in higher education shares a concern with the issue, rooted in their recognition of Japan's economic role in the world. In terms of GDP Japan is comparable to the United States. However, in terms of engagement in scientific research and technological development, the Japanese do not feel fully confident. They may believe that Japan is a world leader in science and technology, but then they ask why so few foreign students seek to enroll in Japanese universities, why academic exchanges are so difficult to sustain, and why masses of researchers have not come to Japan.

The answer is that Japanese universities are not really internationalized. The first question is how to improve them, so that they might attract more foreign students. Common wisdom says that the difficulty of learning the Japanese language is the barrier. In recent years, many efforts have been made to prepare courses taught in English, although these remain just special courses. Only one university identifies itself as a bilingual university. That university was established during the occupation after World War II, with strong American involvement. Even people who are committed to developing courses taught in English would never envision English one day becoming the language of instruction on Japanese campuses, taking the place of their own language. This is the irony: Japan wants to live together with other parts of the world, but it will never give up its culture.

In scientific fields, many scientists publish their papers in English, but the majority of them still write and publish in Japanese. At issue is whether the nation wishes to see all of its researchers write in English. If a referendum were held, the result would probably be "No!" How to maintain the national identity while coping with the power of Western civilization remains the key issue for Japanese education.

If all research were carried out in English and all classes conducted in English, would Japanese institutions be more attractive to the outside world? Conversely, if Japanese universities continue teaching in Japanese will they ever attract more foreigners? To be universal but unique is the difficult task for institutions outside the Western hemisphere.

8.
Current Issues and Future Priorities for European Higher Education Systems

BARBARA SPORN

In their theme chapter, Philip Altbach and Todd Davis outline areas within higher education that are undergoing major changes or profoundly affecting higher education systems around the globe. In Europe, many of the same areas have been discussed and have been targets for reform over the last decade. This chapter outlines major current issues of higher education in selected countries of continental Europe and presents future priorities from a mainly organizational viewpoint.

Current Issues

In general, colleges and universities in continental Europe are facing three major challenges: expansion, diversification, and massification. Expansion refers to the large increases in student numbers in most European countries in response to public policies providing education to a large portion of the population, often under the banner "education for all." For example, in Austria the number of students almost doubled between 1980 and 1995. A second observable trend is diversification. Many nations like Germany, France, or the Netherlands have a binary system of higher and vocational education, which translates into different types of institutions for different target groups. Where this split did not exist (for example, in Austria or Switzerland), governments and ministries have introduced or are planning to implement a more diverse landscape for higher education, in line with the interests and aspirations of potential students. Switzerland is in the process of introducing *Fachhochschulen* (i.e., vocational training institutions) to its system of higher education. A third issue confronting European universities is "massification," which refers to overcrowded and overburdened institutions that are hard to work in, to study in, and to manage. In Germany, unbearable studying conditions—such as lecture classes with over 1,000 students—unavailable professors, and incompetent administrators caused major student strikes in 1998.

These three developments, the result of public (i.e., federal or state) policies, have shaped the problems facing institutions of higher education in Europe: higher education funding (privatization); international reputation (mobility); equal access and diversity; relevance of studies (labor market requirements, graduate education); and the role of the state in relation to institutions (accountability).

The issue of funding national systems of higher education has been a major trigger for restructuring higher education in Europe. One reason has been the push for state budget consolidation to meet unified standards for the introduction of a common currency (the euro) in Europe, starting in 1999. Consequently, the European Union and its member nations had to find ways to cut public spending, and higher education budgets have often been the target for such decreases. Many ministries—and this was the case in Austria—have looked for ways to make universities more efficient. As indicated in the theme chapter, this often leads to strategies of privatization. Colleges and universities should develop their own management structure, set up and revise programs independently, serve society and students as "customers," and attract additional resources.

Funding strategies for higher education have been changing as well. In most countries, budgets in the past were itemized by categories like personnel, libraries, or maintenance. The new trend in many European countries is toward lump sum funding, with the state allocating monies mainly according to output-oriented indicators and formalized planning procedures. These public funds can then be apportioned within institutions according to their particular preferences and strategies. For example, the German and Swedish governments have implemented budget allocation procedures based on the performance of respective colleges and universities in their countries (e.g., data on graduates and publications). In Austria, under the new reform, 85 percent of the university budget is based on the previous year's calculations. The rest is contingent on a state contract defining variable budget needs for projects and outcomes.

Many institutions and nations have placed a priority on creating a more internationally reputed system of higher education through compatible study programs, excellence in research, and high mobility of students and staff. This internationalization of higher education is very relevant for continental Europe. The increased competition in Europe for students and resources has compelled universities to create strategies for improving their image and reputation in specialized fields of research and training. The aim is to enhance the quality of services and in that way move up in the ranks and gain higher visibility.

Mobility has played a key role in this process. Students in European exchange programs (e.g., Socrates, Tempus, ERASMUS) make choices based on their perception of the best campuses and the most supportive faculty, thereby increasing competition among universities. Research through international collaboration and exchanges has to meet certain standards as well. Very often, these standards are defined by the U.S. tradition of refereed journal publishing. Accordingly, many European universities try to encourage their junior faculty to move to other countries and work with international colleagues—in the expectation that when they return to their home institutions, their research productivity, teaching quality, and hence reputation will increase. At the Vienna University of Economics and Business Administration, junior faculty are strongly encouraged (through funds and contacts) to teach and do research in other countries in order to get promoted.

The internationalization of higher education also involves the need for equal access and diversity at European institutions. With new forms of student and staff mobility and migration streams from Eastern Europe and Africa, universities have to accommodate a population more diverse in ethnic and educational background. The expansion in student numbers has boosted this trend even further, creating a situation for which universities are often unprepared. Emerging political and economic changes have put integration of diversity on the agenda in many nations in Europe that are used to a relatively homogeneous society. At the same time, countries like Austria need a large number of well-trained and skilled academics, given the nature of their economies and high standard of living (Austria is the eighth-richest country in the world). With businesses being based on high-end technologies, to qualify for high-salaried positions, graduates need to be well trained. Policies to enhance access and diversity through a binary system, while maintaining quality standards, have characterized Austrian higher education reforms. On top of that, universities are increasingly rewarded for their output (i.e., graduates). The universities need to develop common quality standards, which could prove difficult if the student population becomes more diverse. This is an indication of the multifaceted problems involving access and diversity—especially in combination with educational quality—in many European countries.

In connection with the growing concern over access and diversity, public scrutiny has focused on the relevance of studies and the extent to which they equip students with the necessary knowledge and skills in preparation for the job market. Two initiatives related to these issues are the establishment of the consortium of management schools (CEMS), which offers a joint high-level business degree, and the "Sorbonne declaration" in 1998, which introduced the "baccalaureate" (undergraduate education) as a new common level in Germany, France, Italy, and the United Kingdom. The CEMS degree consists of study periods in different countries, internships in businesses, and requires fluency in two foreign languages. The degree provides students with practical training, international experience, and personal development and has been well received by business employers. The second initiative grew out of discussions in many European nations about harmonizing tier systems by introducing an additional (third) level (i.e., the baccalaureate). The idea was that students should have the possibility of leaving university earlier and still earn a degree. Graduate education (at the master's and Ph.D. level) could follow afterward. To meet the constantly changing needs of the job market, educational institutions need to provide relevant and lifelong learning opportunities to society.

A number of important reforms concern the role of the state and institutions of higher education. The nation-state seems to have outserved its purpose, and its function has been redefined as supervising (as

70

opposed to controlling) higher education development. This is a change from the past, when state ministries were responsible for all areas of higher education—including funding, access policies, program planning, and employment issues involving academics and administration. The move toward a supervisory role for the state led to the introduction of quality standards and external reviews, greater institutional autonomy, buffer organizations, new information flows, and alternative procedures for resource allocation and funding.

What used to be state-run public universities have been "offered" a new degree of freedom. As noted in the chapter by Altbach and Davis, this trend can be viewed as the privatization of the public sector. Autonomy in budgetary, personnel, and programmatic matters increased the need for institutions to learn to manage the enterprise by applying techniques from business. This "managerialism" has characterized many European universities and is reflected in the growing size of administration as opposed to the stagnating size of faculty. Universities are often confronted by the demand to "do more with less": that is, state budgetary support may decline, but institutions should continue to provide quality education to an often growing student body. This social and economic role of universities still needs to develop into a system capable of actually fulfilling the far-reaching expectations of ministries and the general public. Institutional accountability, the use of information technology, and the role of the academic profession are all major areas of transition with which European universities have to cope in the future.

The countries of continental Europe have generally succeeded, through legislation or other measures, in mandating change within their higher education systems. These reforms have undoubtedly been "moving closer to the market." This has been motivated by high drop-out rates, the lengthy time-to-degree, inadequate research productivity, and over-crowded institutions. These inefficiencies, together with tight national budgets, have formed a strong basis for change. Although actions might differ between countries (e.g., in the United Kingdom strengthening state influence, in Sweden weakening state influence) the goals are clear: to create effective educational systems for a diverse group of students at lower cost, to increase the relevance of studies for the job market through efficient training, and to enhance research that is addressing society's problems. The underlying assumption is that market forces will help universities to solve their most pressing problems.

To give some national examples, three geographical areas seem to represent most of what is happening in Europe: the Netherlands, Scandinavia (Sweden, Norway, Denmark, and Finland), and the German-speaking countries (Austria, Switzerland, and Germany). The case of the Netherlands can serve as a model for reforms in other European countries and deserves special attention. In the Netherlands, a binary system of vocational training institutions and research universities has been introduced to channel enrollments and student needs in order to serve the job market. Additionally, quality assessment of educational programs and faculty by external agencies and international peers has been implemented. Institutional autonomy and university management have benefited from new governance and leadership structures. Consequently, Dutch universities abandoned senates and now work simply with a board of directors and trustees (including the president, or rector), the deans of the different schools, and an advisory faculty board.

This Dutch model has been translated into other national settings. In Scandinavia, reforms include a strong emphasis on evaluation and quality management, monitored by external agencies. The emerging pivotal role of academic institutions (as opposed to the state) has emerged through decentralization and institutional self-regulation. In Germany, Austria, and Switzerland the elements have slightly different labels, but similar meanings: privatization (establishment of universities that are legally separate from the state), diversification (a variety of institutional types differentiated by program orientation), performance contracts (funding based on some output measures), and financial autonomy (freedom of internal resource allocation and acquisition).

In this new broader environment of mandates for accountability, efficient and effective education, and international visibility, colleges and universities have been developing specific responses. These include a shift within the internal authority structure toward greater power for the leadership and administration, leaner governance structures (with fewer committees comprised of delegates from the schools and departments), the presence of external interest groups on university boards and decision-making bodies, a stronger focus on the customer (student), and a more integrated organizational structure, introducing institutes encompassing related disciplines.

Future Priorities
In general, continental Europe has been moving in the direction of

market-oriented higher education systems. The central role of academic institutions seems inevitable given the high degree of autonomy and high expectations of accountability. We can discern a number of lines of development.

First, systems and institutions need to "think global and act local" in order to enhance internationalization, while taking regional needs and differences into consideration. Second, the integration of shifting external interests and needs is increasingly important and will require techniques for staying informed about the labor market, the economy, and other important external variables. Third, universities need to implement planning procedures that ensure speed, precision, flexibility, and readiness. Fourth, international exchange and mobility will be critical for graduates to strengthen their qualifications and enhance the sophistication of "soft skills" like intercultural sensitivity, languages, and adaptability. Fifth, expansion and diversification of higher education systems will lead to a push for an even greater division of labor in teaching and research. The old Humdoldtian model of the unity of teaching and research will most probably be abandoned in exchange for building core competencies in applied and basic research and in undergraduate and graduate training. Some European universities (e.g., the University of Twente in the Netherlands, the University of St. Gallen in Switzerland, and the University of Warwick in the United Kingdom) have already realized the potential of building up core competency fields and attracting new audiences and sponsors. Sixth, colleges and universities will increasingly specialize, focusing on what they do best and offering it efficiently and effectively to the market. Large comprehensive universities will be organizations of the past; lean structures with areas of expertise will be the most successful institutions in the future.

If we examine the current organizational forms of these market-oriented higher education systems, we can identify certain barriers to achieving new goals. Their bureaucratic and collegial culture often hinders collaboration, adaptation, and entrepreneurial behavior. New organizational forms might be more effective for creating networks, conglomerates, cultures, strategic alliances, and mergers.

Organizational networks, implemented at universities, might prove advantageous both internally and externally. Internally, different disciplines, academic departments, and administrative units can be linked either through information technology, mission statements, management, or multidisciplinary initiatives. This network approach helps to integrate separate and highly specialized units. Externally, networks set up reliable and reciprocal relationships with partners (or vendors) like state ministries, publishing companies, or schools. This then enhances the development of trust and shared policies of benefit to all partners. Given a tradition of networks based on the disciplines, the new integrated networks are an approach that could be readily implemented in universities.

Conglomerates as a new organizational form for universities could be initiated by current diversification of higher education systems and the resulting need on the part of institutions to match up with different market segments. Instead of offering "everything for everybody" or "more of the same," academic organizations will increasingly find new ways to differentiate their services based on market needs (e.g., vocational training, continuing education, research university elements, consulting, and technology transfer). For example, in a major step, the Vienna University of Economics and Business Administration will develop a new "differentiated" structure divided into vocational, research, and continuing education. The conglomerate institution, held together under one umbrella, could become a viable model for the future of European universities.

Organizational culture can serve as another principle for building colleges and universities. Through a system of shared values, consisting of common norms, organizational behavior becomes geared more uniformly toward a common good and set of goals. Conflicts between groups within institutions caused by the push for greater market orientation, restructured governance structures, or shifting authority relations can be overcome by fostering a common organizational culture with which most can identify.

Strategic alliances are already in place at many European colleges and universities. Gaining competitive advantage and the chance to cut costs and attract new "customers" have motivated the creation of contracts and arrangements among different universities in Europe (and also in the United States). Strategic benefits range from increased income, greater visibility, and improved services. For example, the Vienna University of Economics and Business Administration has been successfully offering an IMBA degree (International Master of Business Administration) together with the University of South Carolina for many years and thereby attracting an international student body but also bypassing legal restrictions on public universities in Austria.

Another organizational form that comes to mind—analogous to recent trends in private industry—are institutional mergers. The market concentration observed in the oil, entertainment, and banking industries could also hit higher education systems. Some examples already point in that direction. In 1997, Stanford University and the University of California at San Francisco merged their hospitals and clinics. More recently, in November 1998, Western Governors University and the U.S. branch of the Open University in the United Kingdom (both distance education institutions) entered into a cooperative arrangement, called the Governors Open University System; students can earn credits for courses at both institutions. This trend could progress even further to complete takeovers or mergers of entire universities, with the goal of increasing market share and control and reducing costs. The consequences for the academic profession, the structure of educational programs, and the social role of universities would be dramatic; such an approach would require further research.

The University of the Future
My analysis has focused mainly on an institutional perspective and has referred to existing research findings (Clark 1998; Slaughter and Leslie 1997; Sporn 1999). The underlying goal of the higher education reforms is to increase flexibility and adaptability in order to survive in an internationally competitive market.

It might be useful to speculate on how the university of the future might look. Academic units like departments or institutes would be motivated to redefine their roles and responsibilities within the institution. In this setting, academic freedom would be used to meet the needs and expectations of external and internal constituencies, and would serve the interests of the institution rather than the disciplines. Through shared governance, professional management, and committed leadership, a "triangle of partnership" could be formed between administration and faculty. Administrations increasingly use management techniques to run institutions and to support core academic activities.

Through wide-ranging participation of all major groups in a model of shared governance, important and critical decisions could be made and implemented more easily. Committed leaders would provide the necessary financial and visionary support for change and adaptation.

From a structural perspective, the university of the future could be differentiated into core competencies—for example, applied and basic research or continuing and vocational education. A focused mission could integrate these areas on an institutional level and provide direction and the overall goals toward which the university was developing. Diversified funds could be acquired through these differentiated activities and used at the institution's discretion. Altogether, this new university would be characterized by an entrepreneurial culture in which all members work in accordance with changing environmental demands and for the common institutional good.

The functions of this new university would include efficient and effective decision making ("doing the right things and doing them right") through the reduced size of governing bodies and the participation of external interest group representatives. Additionally, advisory steering bodies would help in strategic policymaking, where these are boards of trustees or similar arrangements. For example, in Austria, the most recent reform plans to introduce a steering body for each university, consisting of external groups responsible for supervising budget and personnel planning as well as for electing the rector and vice-rectors. Consultation, dialogue, and consensus would continue to be traditions within institutions of higher education. But they would be used to serve the new functions of the university and engage administration, faculty, students, and external constituencies on equal terms.

Regarding services of the new university, the amount of interdisciplinary research would become the key measure for funding and promotion of specific academic units, which would lead to new partnerships with industry and other groups in society. At the same time, relevance and quality of studies would remain a top priority for most European colleges and universities. Programs focused on specific job markets, general education including personal development, and lifelong learning opportunities could develop and improve. Altogether, transparency of processes, internally and externally, would help to fulfill the expectations of society and the public for accountability and responsibility of institutions of higher education.

In the coming millennium European higher education will undergo a complex and stressful set of changes. On the one hand, state budget constraints are not going to disappear in the short term. Hence, universities will need to find new sources of funding, which will require in-depth analysis of performance in teaching and research. It seems that most countries are looking for "organizational" solutions—that is, new structures and processes for efficiency and effectiveness. On the other hand, problems will arise as a consequence of this restructuring. Shifting authority structures between administration and faculty, the changing role of professors as service providers, and the differences in the attractiveness of various disciplines and fields will lead to major internal conflicts. It remains to be seen how the universities of the 21st century can keep their traditional role as a place for liberal education and reconcile that role with market requirements.

These future priorities certainly imply challenges and call for action. A new knowledge industry will include many more institutions competing for resources and customers. Hence, a redefinition of the roles of constituencies (faculty, administration, students) in decision making, of knowledge discovery and dissemination, and of educational programs will form future focal points for strategic planning at European universities. Most important, student learning as an indicator for efficiency and effectiveness will be measured by social demand and employment opportunities. In summary, Europe is facing dramatic shifts in what used to be model higher education systems for the rest of the world.

References
Clark, B. R. 1998. Creating entrepreneurial universities. Oxford: Pergamon.
Slaughter, S., and L. L. Leslie. 1997. Academic capitalism: Politics, policies, and the entrepreneurial university. Baltimore: Johns Hopkins University Press.
Sporn, B. 1999. Adaptive university structures: An analysis of ad aptation to socioeconomic environments of U.S. and European universities. London: Jessica Kingsley.

9.

A Regional Perspective:
CENTRAL AND EASTERN EUROPE

PETER DARVAS

In the last decade, higher education has emerged as a key sector in the social and economic transition taking place in the countries of Central and Eastern Europe and of the former Soviet Union. The concerns of the public and of politicians have focused on higher education in a number of ways. First, these societies suffered a critical loss of intellectual resources due to national disintegration, political purges, brain drain, and market restructuring. Second, in all these countries, higher education has provided an important recruitment base for the newly emerging political arena. Faculty and students have become part of a new breed of public personalities, which allows representatives of the sector to gain more influence and thus retain or even enhance their political privileges. Third, higher education is increasingly seen (realistically or with ideological overtones) as a leading force to help transitional societies catch up with wealthy nations. Finally, in many countries, higher education as a sector has experienced deprivation and crisis, given the problems of feasibility and sustainability. In countries that have gone through civil conflicts and violent confrontations, the resulting physical destruction has made costly rehabilitation programs necessary that are hardly feasible. In countries that have experienced economic and financial deterioration, the inadequately maintained infrastructure and devalued salaries have left higher education in turmoil, as sustaining quality or even basic services does not seem possible.

In spite of all the attention focused on higher education, it is a sector in which reforms have either failed, were cut short, or simply ignored. Higher education in the region continues to face many critical issues: financial constraints, structural problems, and questions of function and identity. Meanwhile, policymaking, expert analysis, and public discourse are filled with imported preconceptions, political posturing, and global fads—applied in haste, often without local assessment and adaptation (e.g., TQM, to name just one). As a result, reform policies often fail or are compromised; local policy experts suffer a loss of confidence; disappointment sets in because reforms are short lived; apathy grows because of the lack of dynamism in higher education; and centralization and corruption reappear.

The Limited Relevance of Global Issues and Trends

Before looking at the substantive issues reflecting global convergence, we need to reflect on our approach to these issues. With few exceptions, analysis of higher education in the region has produced a largely uniform or overly generalized understanding of trends, at the expense of acquiring the tools of local assessment and adaptation of reform methods. There seems to be a simplistic progression from trends to policies, importation of some concepts without testing their relevance or without adapting them to the local situation.

Furthermore, the collective thinking seems to revere the experience of the front-runners in higher education development—that is, those countries with the highest enrollment levels and those able to spend significantly more in absolute terms on higher education. Experts offer these experiences as the models to follow, based on the belief in the linear course of higher education development. However, experience in transitional countries suggests that no such linear evolution exists and also that some institutional and systemic challenges in transitional societies exceed anything advanced countries have ever faced.

Countries in the region lack an open and transparent higher education policy arena that might encourage the main actors to act accountably and responsively. Among the most attractive developments in Western (mostly Anglo-Saxon) countries is the advanced level of public forums and public discussion on higher education, which bring together policymakers, researchers, politicians, practitioners, and lay actors. This development, which helps to form public opinion, is often absent from the list of necessary changes in higher education in the region. Yet, stimulating such a process (i.e., developing instruments to make higher education a public concern) could significantly contribute to the reform effort.

Internationalization—including exchange programs, the import and export of advanced knowledge, franchises, etc.—appears to be a means for moving beyond national and institutional borders and thus to globalize higher education (setting global standards and policies). However, internationalization may also be a way to revive or save academia in the face of the above-mentioned challenges—mainly restriction of resources and lack of sustainability.

Issues that appear to reflect some global convergence of systems and policies may actually conceal opposing or conflicting trends. For instance, privatization of higher education in Central Asia may have altogether different causes and effects than in Western Europe.

Higher education is almost unique in the sense that global challenges and global dynamics affect systems and institutions having vastly different unit costs—that is, differences in per capita spending on higher education. Meanwhile global trends and challenges also impact the everyday functioning of higher education everywhere (i.e., through shared expectations, standards, concepts of quality and excellence, the global academic marketplace, and mobility, etc.). The labor market resembles, in this sense, higher education, although multinational companies and foreign investments appear to be more active, if not more effective, in balancing out the inequalities of the markets.

Converging Trends and Policy Consequences
Convergence in institutional patterns, transition to mass systems, and funding challenges are clearly observable across continents. Along with the emergence of similar or comparable types of social demand, however, many of these global phenomena may be explained by shared sources of information. Higher education, both institutions and individuals, have relatively easy access to expert information on what works and for what reason. The converging trends, however, need to be looked at with some caution.

The postcommunist transition of Central and Eastern European societies drew considerable attention and support from the international community of donors and experts. Higher education reform gained its appropriate share of attention. The countries in the region that have fallen behind global norms or appear to lack a coherent understanding of the issues have attracted abundant advice and consultation. The two most frequently visited subjects are expansion and finance.

Countries frequently and legitimately compare the growth rates of their higher education systems against international trends. However, the relationship between growth, diversification of programs, and institutional development is less frequently analyzed or considered. Expansion can have a very different cause, character, and impact—depending on social and economic development. Historically, the growth in student numbers in the United States was preceded by diversification and institutionalization of advanced knowledge; whereas in Western Europe, expansion was stimulated by social demand upon a resistant academia. In Central and Eastern Europe, increasing demand—still heavily limited by selection and other forms of control—is occurring at a time when the traditional institutional structure of universities is declining, if not disintegrating. Quality control is often limited to the desire of traditional universities to protect themselves, sometimes by limiting the ability of new institutions to gain accreditation and to compete within the system. Meanwhile, new institutions try to offer new programs without adequate resources or quality assurances. In this situation, increasing access would (or does) only mean access to degrees, as a substitute for access to higher learning.

In terms of funding, countries like the United States, Australia, or New Zealand have played leading roles in designing schemes and involving users in new arrangements (tuition fees, loans, vouchers, etc.). This has perhaps led to a perception that national wealth and the expansion of higher education and institutional diversity (in the area of finance, as well) are interrelated. However, while the wealthy countries in the West managed to retain significant public funding for higher education, countries in Central and Eastern Europe or Central Asia have had to raise a major portion of their revenues from nonstate sources. In the region, it appears that the poorer a country is, the more it is forced to charge user fees, which contributes to increasing inequality and often corruption. Tuition-charging systems often lack the resources to create programs (e.g., loans and scholarships) to balance out the unintended social consequences of tuition fees. Meanwhile, in countries where a full tuition fee system has not been introduced, revenues are often raised through nonaccountable, corrupt ways—either by institutions (charging illegal tuition fees) or by individual staff (selling admissions on an individual basis).

The Changing Relationship between Higher Education and Work

The theme chapter correctly points to the link between education and work as a leading issue of global concern. I would like to add two points to this discussion: first, how past experiences from the region show the inappropriateness of systemic approaches and, second, the extent to which present experiences show the inadequacies of institutional strategies.

Planning the relationship between higher education and work on the basis of the trained-manpower needs of emerging industries was the cornerstone of the approach of communist governments. It took two decades to recognize that planning on a systemic level could not combat the problem that the educational cycle differed markedly in its timing and range from the work cycle. Governments still try to control and influence educational inputs at the national level through selection at the secondary level; outputs they try to control through close supervision of content. (One need not look at Soviet-type systems to find examples of such an approach.) However, governments cannot contain the volatility of labor markets or the dynamics of an ever more globalizing economic system.

The postcommunist transition brought about, among other things, disenchantment regarding planning. Incremental allocation of funding and the scarcity of admissions places have sustained a relatively comfortable strategic position for the institutions that are not motivated to engage in strategic planning. Most institutions are almost tenaciously and protectively relying on their traditional privileges and structures. They ignore challenges expressed in the form of social and economic demand. These institutions are set up to protect the authority and autonomy of advanced knowledge, even in the face of the vicissitudes of contested financial systems. However, the institutions are not set up to address new challenges from the economy and from labor markets.

The increasing demand for higher education has brought about the need for new programs either through in-country-based innovation or through international assistance and program development. The countries of the region display an impressive number of new programs, innovative initiatives—ranging from immediately marketable business and management schools to institutions with nontraditional curricula and methods of delivery. For the policy-research dialogue, the main challenge stems from the fact that innovative local centers, wishing to produce new knowledge, rarely possess adequate intellectual resources or the funds to make the necessary investments, cover the upfront expenses of new institutions, or even sustain programs in the medium term. Although Western capital rushed in to invest in business ventures, private investors or multinational companies have not yet invested in human capital development on an adequate level, comparable to similar investments in the West.

Meanwhile, countries and regions in need of new advanced programs can become new markets for the educationally and economically better-established Western institutions and educational communities. New distance-learning courses, exchange programs, foreign franchises, and information-technology-based learning opportunities have mushroomed across the region. The main risk is that such new programs often do not address the problems of sustainability, long-term impact, or stimulating local innovation and adaptation. Discussion, analysis, and strategy might shed light on issues like feasible new structures, sustainable new institutions (alternatives to the traditional universities), and strategies to generate new local educational resources. As an example, more research and discussion should focus on the impact, effectiveness, and feasibility of training new trainers.

One of the critical issues around the education-work transition is the increasing demand for lifelong learning opportunities. This demand is also apparent in developing and transitional societies, although more as an implicit need on the part of employers rather than as a manifest and sustainable demand by employees. Learning opportunities beyond the school system are not only far from being on the rise, but they are in a deeper crisis than is the school system itself. Predictably, potential providers (i.e., members of the corporate sector, local government agencies, nongovernmental organizations, or revenue-seeking schools) will need a longer period to devise and consolidate their strategies.

The critical and immediate systemic issues for reform-oriented governments are how to restructure the school system so that it "produces" candidates for lifelong learning; how to provide society with the skills to adapt to changing environments; how to find the proper balance between vocational and general content; how to offer choices among multiple types of educational career; and how to facilitate transitions, modifications, exit, and reentry into the school system. In higher education, related issues would be the emerging need for short-cycle programs, postsecondary forms, shorter first-degree programs based on the credit system and student choice, non-Ph.D. advanced (second-degree) programs, and new forms of adult training and retraining—all of which need to be designed and promoted in response to local demand and by using local resources.

The Changing Face of Higher Education:
The Emergence of New Stakeholders
The theme chapter discusses a number of global issues—including privatization, access, equity, and accountability. The transformation of higher education in Central and Eastern Europe has occurred within a relatively short period and has been intimately connected with broader social and economic changes. All of these interrelated issues represent aspects of a systemic change in which new stakeholders emerge or the social and economic position of old ones undergoes a radical change.

The main underlying trend appears to be a changing perception of higher education relative to the private/public dilemma. Historically, the public provision and ownership of higher education in the region meant a state-protected privilege for the internal actors (students, faculty, and institutions). That privilege is being mostly secured by defining higher education as a public or state service.

Higher education traditionally was used to recruit the small governmental elite, some leading professions, and an industrial elite, as well as to provide vocational skills for those who were selected to carry out the state's industrialization policies. Higher education did not assist in the development of an educationally conscious middle class, one that would have been able to devise its educational strategies in terms of individual well-being and success and to pressure higher education accordingly. Such an expanding middle class emerged in most Western countries between the 1940s and 1960s. Increasingly, higher education became a channel into public and private employment and, more generally, a means to improve individual well-being. Middle-class demand for higher education was based partly on the private needs of the individual beneficiaries of the training and of private employers, who provide the jobs and demand for technological advancements.

In Central and Eastern Europe well-being has been only loosely connected to educational attainment, since the financial rewards of education were not evident. Careers are controlled through organizational and political loyalty as much as through training and specialization. Higher education as a private good has not been distinguished from higher education as a public good. The private interests of the beneficiaries were subordinated to public interests, which included limits on admissions, restricted program structures, and strict certification requirements.

During the 1990s, this picture has been radically altered by social policies and pressures to increase enrollments and admit larger cohorts of the population. Each country in the region drafted policies to increase student numbers significantly, to at least 15 to 25 percent per age group by 2001. These plans are the first steps toward a massification of higher education and diversification of academic programs. They are also aimed at meeting a broader range of social demands. This projected growth will pose a major challenge to higher educational institutions. Higher education gained its reputation not as much through its high standards of instruction or research but through its exclusivity; it has been more difficult to gain entry into the system than to stay in it. Its value originated from its scarcity. As access becomes more open, higher education will need new sources of external prestige.

One of the major problems institutions will face is the changing articulation between secondary and higher education. An increase in higher education enrollments in Central and Eastern Europe may be limited by the size and structure of secondary education. While admissions rates to higher education may be radically increased, it will be difficult to follow this with a similar rate of expansion at the secondary level. Furthermore, secondary schooling faces its own challenge from a restructuring labor market. As a result, the qualifications and expectations of those leaving secondary schools and seeking to enter higher education will be more diverse. This will pose a major challenge to the traditionally elitist higher educational systems.

Under these circumstances, private initiatives are responding not just to qualitative but rather mostly to quantitative demand. Unlike in the United States, for instance, private institutions in the region do not necessarily offer higher-quality programs, often quite the reverse. Meanwhile, they depend more on tuition fees than do private institutions in the United States, as state support or alternate funding sources are not easy to gain access to. Private institutions typically offer vocational degrees in high-demand fields, such as computer science, economics and management, or foreign languages. These are also usually not fields over which academic or professional elites can exercise much in the way of formal regulations. As a consequence, criticism of privatization could also be explained as the attempt by insiders to protect their privileges. Access to the public system has been a way of controlling entry into the privileged elite; selection is the instrument to check this recruitment.

At present, the pressure to expand the system has coincided with the increasing impoverishment of large segments of society. Therefore, the growing number of first-year admissions does not necessarily mean an opening up of the system to a sufficiently large cohort of the population. In addition, in many countries from Central Europe to Central Asia, there has been a radical reemergence of ethnic problems: in some countries, new states and borders have created new challenges; in others, reinvigorated ethnic identities have stimulated calls for more opportunities of higher learning. Neither the relative opening of access to publicly subsidized places, nor privatization has effectively assisted these groups to gain better access to higher education and ensure that a higher proportion of their members attain higher degrees. Mobility stimulated by education appears to be conspicuously low in transitional and developing countries. Meanwhile, the private returns from higher education have steadily increased in the same transitional societies—further contributing to a widening gap between affluent and the low-income groups, as well as between the ethnic majorities and minorities.

The lack of open access to publicly subsidized higher education services has raised the question of who controls the sector and the spending of public (taxpayer-paid) monies. However, higher education is still considered an internal matter for academics, and decisions are still based on the academic ethos.

Although the trend toward managerialism has also reached most countries of the region, a great deal of control is still exercised by the academic profession, not as much through peer-based activities and restrictions on selection and recruitment as by means of holding senior positions in institutions as well as in government.

87

There is now an increasing demand in the region for a clear separation between institutional management and the professorial or academic power of the faculty. This separation will contribute to the breaking up of traditional forms of institutional hierarchy, in which the academic prestige and authority translated directly into organizational prestige and authority. Traditional authorities and collective decision-making bodies and councils will not be able to maintain effective and impartial control over the "business administration" of the institutions.

Conclusion

The higher educational systems of the countries in Central and Eastern Europe and the former Soviet Union are in a period of identity crisis. Social and economic pressures have risen at a time when the regulatory and financial means of the state, the sole actor of policymaking in the past, have been weakened or eliminated. Even the pressure groups are in transition and in conflict with one another: elites and ethnic majorities defend their interest sphere against diversity, academics protect their turf against external interests and lay control. Terms such as quality, efficiency, accountability, and equity have lost their solid context and new ones are being sought. International influence, exchanges, and partnerships may have a place in identity formation as the structures and institutions of higher education—disciplinary, vertical, and horizontal—will be pressed to follow international trends.

Under these conditions, an international partnership is more than just an opportunity. Since institutional leaders and academics may no longer be able to sustain themselves or even cover the basic necessities, they will need to turn to international funding, exchanges, and partnerships. A distance-education program or an international research endeavor is a way of bringing in basic resources. The challenge stems from the fact that international research requires a great deal of adaptation and local learning before it is applicable: defining new rules of governance, quality control, or financial administration depends on local needs, capabilities, and social dynamics. New developments—often based on international sponsorship, cooperation, or exchange—will need to be sustained. Over the last few years, several initiatives have brought together policymakers, researchers, and practitioners. Most of these, however, were concluded after one meeting, and at best they resulted in the publication of a new book. Whereas scholarly dissemination is important, the sustainability of such initiatives is critical.

Examples abound, but let me cite only one: when international partnerships bring North American liberal arts traditions to Eastern Europe to rescue the curriculum of first-degree programs in higher education, one must carefully assess the social environment with respect to capacities and impact.

Contributors

Philip G. Altbach is J. Donald Monan, S.J. professor of higher education and director of the Center for International Higher Education at Boston College. He is author of *Comparative Higher Education* and other books. He serves as the editor of *The Review of Higher Education*.

Patti McGill Peterson is executive director of the Council for the International Exchange of Scholars (Fulbright Program) and vice president of the Institute of International Education. She has been president of St. Lawrence University and of Wells College.

Nasima Badsha is deputy director for higher education in the Department of Education, Government of South Africa.

Suma Chitnis is executive director of the Tata Endowment for the Education of Indians, Mumbai, India. She has been vice chancellor of SNDT University, Mumbai, India, and has taught at the Tata Institute of Social Science.

Peter Darvas is senior education specialist at the World Bank, Washington, D.C. He has been director of the Higher Education Support Program of the Open Society Institute, Budapest, Hungary.

Todd M. Davis is director of research at the Institute of International Education, New York.

George S. Eshiwani is vice chancellor of Kenyatta University, Nairobi, Kenya. He has taught at the University of Nairobi and Jomo Kenyatta University of Agriculture and Technology.

Allan Goodman is president and chief executive officer of the Institute of International Education, New York.

Weifang Min is executive vice president of Peking University, Beijing, China. He has been assistant to the chancellor of the University of Texas System. Dr. Min currently serves as vice president of the China Higher Education Research Association.

Akimasa Mitsuta is professor in the School of International Studies at Obirin University, Tokyo, Japan. He has served as a senior official in the Japanese Ministry of Education.

Simon Schwartzman is director of the Center for Social Research on Sustainable Development in Rio de Janeiro, a partnership between the Brazilian Foundation for Sustainable Development and the American Institutes for Research. He has been president of the Brazilian Foundation for Geography and Statistics and has been on the faculty at the University of Campinas, Brazil.

Barbara Sporn is assistant professor in the Department of Management Information Systems at the Vienna University of Economics and Business Administration (*Wirtschaftsuniversität Wien*). She has been visiting professor at Stanford University.